To Bill Hastings

A famous
name "Hastings" in the
area. please enjoy
this little history of
our area.

Robert
Bunting

Robert Bunting

MW00632527

INTO OBLIVION

The Lives and Times Leading up to the Final Voyage of the Steamship Marine City from the Ghost Town of Alcona, Michigan on Lake Huron, 1880

By
Robert Lowell Bunting
September 12, 2007

Published by
Black River Trading Company, LTD.
Oxford, Michigan and Downton, England
ISBN No. 978-0-9797492-0-9
Library of Congress Control Number: 2007904636
Copyright Number: TXu1 – 353-158

All that is important to you will cease to exist....
Old Buddhist saying

Acknowledgement

All that remains of her are some broken timbers and rough, twisted and rusted metal work peering above the waves along a sugar sand beach. The attempt to recreate what the Steamer *Marine City* looked like and what the once vibrant Northern Michigan Town of Alcona was took us on a marvelous journey into the past. Sources included newspapers such as the Toledo Blade and Alcona County Review; London Archives; City of Marine City Archives; U.S. Life Saving Service Archives; U.S. Coast Guard Archives; the National Oceanic and Atmospheric Administration; the National Archives and Records Administration documents; Lloyds of London Insurance records in London, England; salvage divers; historians including Doris Gauthier of Harrisville, Michigan; locals; shipbuilders; the Great Lakes Maritime Institute; Dossin Museum of Detroit; many and various other reference media sources; folklore; and oral histories. We cannot vouch for the accuracy of all of the following information as it comes sometimes from sources that are difficult, if not impossible, to substantiate 125-150 years later.

I wish to express deep appreciation to Robin L. Schmidt of the Law Firm of Robert L. Bunting who dedicated many hours over three years doing historical research, including deciphering old handwritten accounts barely legible while engaged as Researcher for my Law Firm.

I want to thank those interested in Alcona and the shipwreck of the Marine City whose help and abiding enthusiasm were of great assistance to me. They are Joseph F. Kosik Sr., Ron Citkowski, Ron D. Gauthier, Judy Riley, Jeremy Dobry, Erica Flock of the Alcona County Review, William Carlson, Don Sawyer and Gordon Bennett III, the latter two having served as Presidents of the Alcona Historical Society and my personal secretary Sara A. Bejma.

We are all very grateful to Robert McGreevy for bringing to bear his considerable maritime artistic talent and assisting the research efforts in painting the Steamship *Marine City* and the Town of Alcona in all their splendor based on the historical record uncovered here. Mr. McGreevy's rendition of the town of Alcona with the famous tugboat *Vulcan* alongside the hefty Alcona Pier is superb and accurate. It was based on old maps, plats, directories and accounts of the Town and its heavy docking capabilities, all of which proved invaluable after an exhaustive

4

and unsuccessful search for old photographs, tintypes and daguerreotypes. He also did the illustration of the Hackett medal awarded to Captain Thomas Hackett of the Tug *Vulcan* for this captain's heroic efforts to save the crew and passengers of the *Marine City*. But for the dedication of these people, the *Marine City*, the Tug *Vulcan* and the ghost town of Alcona would have been lost to history.

Most importantly, I want to thank my wife, Jane, who is amused by my projects and offers helpful insight, and to the Steamship Marine City, the "Lady of the Lake."

Where once stood civilization and its shrill boasts of progress, now the sands of time gently sweep over the hefty works of man and only the lightest tracks of mice go anywhere.

Robert L. Bunting
Harrisville, Michigan 2007

THE STEAMER MARINE CITY

When a steamer came into a remote northern Port of the Great Lakes in the 1800s, it was an event. New people, often foreign immigrants, as well as returning familiar faces, arrived full of promise and wonderment and news of the outside world. They brought the stories of friends and the world beyond to the isolated towns of the North.

The following are accounts from one such traveler:

> It is a luxury to sail on Lake Huron and watch the northern lights...It is spectacular and pleasant to say the least on upon these calm, freshwater seas....

And later in a storm:

> We could scarcely see each other's faces except for the lightning and our ship ground and dragged her anchor in the storms so we dropped the second. In twenty minutes, the sun gilded the shoreline, its forest and we saw an immense herd of wild horses scampering and whisking their long tails. A cloud of pigeons, in countless thousands, shadowing alternately the forest, the lake, and the prairie behind blocked the newly shining sun after the storm; we then saw an extensive encampment of wild Indians along the Michigan shore. It was a dark curtain, that storm, which lifted upon a scene

of wild and singular beauty. [1]

Traveling to America by steamship in the mid-1800s, Charles Dickens made the following observations upon entering his shipboard stateroom in *American Notes for General Circulation:*

That this stateroom had been specially engaged for "Charles Dickens, Esq. and lady" was rendered sufficiently clear even to my scared intellect by a very small manuscript, announcing the fact, which was pinned on a very flat quilt, covering a very thin mattress spread like a surgical plaster on a most inaccessible shelf....... That this utterly impracticable, thoroughly hopeless, and profoundly preposterous box, this stateroom had the remotest reference to, or connection with, those chaste and pretty, not to say gorgeous little sketches made by masterly hand in varnished lithograph hanging in an agent's office..... That this room of state, in short, could be anything but a pleasant fiction and cheerful jest of the Captain's, invented and put in practice for the better relish and enjoyment of the real stateroom presently to be disclosed....these were truths which I really could not for the moment, bring my mind at all to bear upon or comprehend. And I sat down upon a kind of horsehair slab, or perch, of which there were two within; and

[1] *The Making of Michigan 1820-1860 A Pioneer Anthology*, edited by Justin L. Kestenbaum, Wayne State University Press, 1990.

looked, without any expression of countenance whatever, at some friends that had come on board with us, and who were crushing their faces into all manner of shapes by endeavoring to squeeze them through the small doorway into this very, very small area....one of our friends who had made the arrangements for our voyage, turned pale on entering, and retreated on the friend behind him, smote his head involuntarily, and said below his breath, "impossible! It cannot be!" or words to that effect...., It was rather dark, certainly; but somebody said, "of course it will be light at sea" a proposition to which we all assented; echoing "of course, of course" though it would be exceedingly difficult to say why we thought so.

Envisioning a mulled claret wine....

This stateroom now started to grow pretty fast in the company of my friends; but by this time it had expanded into something quite bulky, and almost boasted a bay window to view the sea from. So we went upon the deck again in high spirits; and there, everything was in such a state of bustle and active preparation, that the blood quickened its pace, and whirled through one's veins on that clear frosty morning with involuntary mirthfulness. For every gallant ship was riding slowly up and down, and every little boat was splashing noisily in the water; and lots of people stood upon the wharf gazing with a kind of "dread delight" on the far-famed fast American steamer; and one party of men were "taking in the milk" or, in other words, getting the cow onboard.... And another were filling the very throat of the ship with fresh provisions; with butchers' meat and garden stuff, pale suckling pigs, calves' heads in scores, beef, veal, pork, poultry, etc. and others were coiling rope and busy with oakum yarns and others were lowering heavy packages into the hold and the cursor's head was barely visible as it loomed in a state of exquisite perplexity from the midst of a vast pile of passengers' luggage and there seemed to be nothing going on anywhere, or uppermost in the mind of anybody, but preparations for this mighty voyage.

Later on passage outbound:

I crept below at midnight from the deck. It was not exactly comfortable below....it was decidingly close; it was impossible to be unconscious while the presence of the extraordinary compound of strange smells, which was to be found nowhere but onboard ship, and which is such a subtle perfume that it seems to enter at every pore of the skin, and whisper of the hold.... Every plank and timber creaked as if the ship were made of wicker-wood and now cracked, like an enormous fire of the driest possible twigs.

I am awakened out of sleep by a dismal shriek from my wife, who demands to know whether there's any danger. I arouse myself, and look out of bed. The water-jug is plunging and leaping like a lively dolphin; all the smaller articles are afloat, except my shoes, which are stranded on a carpet bag, high and dry, like a couple of coal barges. Suddenly I see them spring into the air and behold the looking glass which is nailed to the wall, sticking fast upon the ceiling. The same time the door entirely disappears and a new one is opened in the floor. Then I begin to comprehend that the stateroom is standing on its head.

Before it is possible to make any arrangements at all compatible with this novel state of things, the ship rights. Before one can say 'thank Heaven!: she wrongs again. Before one can cry she is wrong, she seems to have started forward, and to be a creature actually running of its own accord, with broken knees and failing legs, through every variety of hole and pitfall, and stumbling constantly. Before one can make so much as wonder, she takes a high leap into the air. Before she has well done that, she takes a deep dive into the water. Before she has gained the surface, she throws a summerset. The instant she is on her legs, she rushes backwards. And so she goes on staggering, heaving, wrestling, leaping, diving, jumping, pitching, throbbing, rolling, and rocking: in going through all these movements, sometimes by turns, and sometimes altogether: until one feels disposed to roar for mercy. A steward passes. "Steward! Sir? What is

11

the matter? What do you call this? Rather a heavy sea on, sir, and a headwind." Imagine the wind howling, the sea roaring, the rain beating: all in a furious array against her. Picture the sky both dark and wild, and the clouds, in fearful symphony with the waves, making another ocean in the air. Add to all this the clattering on deck and down below; the tread of hurried feet; the loud hoarse shouts of seamen; the gurgling in and out of water through the scuppers; with, every now and then, the striking of a heavy sea upon the planks above, and with the deep, dead, heavy sound of thunder heard within a vault, and there is the headwind. I say nothing of what may be called the domestic noises of the ship; such as the breaking of glass and crockery, the tumbling down of stewards, the gambols, overhead, of loose casks and truant dozens of bottled porter, and very remarkable and far from exhilarating sounds raised in the various staterooms by the passengers who were too ill to get up to breakfast, I say nothing of them: although I lay listening to this concert for three or four days, I don't think I heard it for more than a quarter of a minute, at the expiration of each turn, I lay down again, excessively sea-sick.

The laboring of the ship and the troubled sea of this night I shall never forget. "Will it ever be worse than this?" was a question I had often heard asked, when everything was sliding and bumping about, and when it certainly

12

seemed difficult to comprehend the possibility of anything afloat be more disturbed, without toppling over and going down. But what the agitation of steam vessel is, on a bad night on the wild sea, it is impossible for the most vivid imagination to conceive. To say that she is flung down on her side in the waves, and that....spring up again she rolls over on the other side until the heavy waves strike her with the noise of a hundred great guns and hurls her back.... That she stops, and staggers and shivers, as though stung, and then with a violent throbbing at her heart, darts onward like a monster goateed into madness, to be beaten down, and battered, and crushed and leaped on by the angry sea-that thunder, lightening, hail and rain and wind all are in fierce contention for the mastery that every plank has its groan, every nail its shriek and every drop of water in the great rolling sea with its howling voice. To say that all is grand, and all appalling and horrible in the last degree, is nothing. Words cannot express it. Thoughts cannot convey it. Only a dream can call it up again, in all its fury, rage and passion. About midnight we shipped an entire wave, which forced its way through the skylights, burst open the doors above and came raging and roaring down into our cabin, and to the unspeakable...., Of the outrageous antics performed by that ship.... which made a bed a practical joke....but anything like the utter dreariness and desolation that met my eyes when I literally tumbled up on deck... I never saw a horizon....It were all one dull, heavy uniform lead color both water and sky. There was no extend or prospect over the dreary waste that lay around us for the sea ran high and the horizon encompassed us like a black hoop.... Seen from the wet and rolling decks, it only impressed one giddily and painfully. In the gale of last night the lifeboat had been crushed by one blow like a walnut shell and there it hang dangling in the air a mere faggot of crazy boards....A gloomier picture would be hard to look upon.[2]

On arrival at port, however, the steamer whistle was a sound of optimism and new things – a beckoning sound. The steamer carried freight, replenishments of supplies and manufactured goods including woodstoves for cooking and heating during the cold winters.[3] It also brought inventions, as well, such as the bicycle. Townspeople would drop what they were doing to meet the steamer. One such steamer was the *Marine City*, a side-wheeler and a grand ship indeed. She was known as the "Lady of the Lake."

Having started full passenger service in 1875 under Captain William Comer[4], the *Marine City* was a versatile wooden side-

[2] Dickens, Charles. *American Notes for General Circulation,* 1843.
[3] Detroit was the largest manufacturer in the U.S. of wood stoves from 1865 to 1910. Previously it had been the largest maker of cigars with many cigar rolling factories. It was called the "Tampa of the North."
[4] *Shingle Shavers and Berry Pickers* by Oliver Raymond, Raymond, 1976

wheel steamer with her hull originally built in Marine City, Michigan in 1866 by TG Lester and Co. to serve as a large seaworthy barge.

A year later she became a fully operational passenger ship with staterooms and a dining room. She could service smaller coastal ports. She was powered with a walking beam steam engine purchased from the Steamer Ark (formerly the Steamer E.K. Collins). With a powerful, reliable steam engine, the *Marine City* was a capable passenger ship that also carried abundant freight, while making speeds up to 12 knots. She was 192'1" long, 27'9" wide, 10'8" draft, with a 10' deep hold topped with four-6" oak planks and weighing 695 gross tons. Built up into a passenger vessel by P.L. Lester and Arnold Company of Marine City, Michigan, her U.S. Registration number was 16447.

The *Marine City* was the flagship of several package freight and passenger ships sailing under the flag of the People's Line. The People's Line was a profitable shipping line based out of London, England with a Michigan based operating company known as the Michigan Transportation Company. Its Captain, William Comer, had been the captain of other steamships, including: the *Flora*, the *Forrester* and the *Suzanne B. Ward*.[5]

The *Marine City* and her sister ships serviced the coastal communities of Lake

---

[5] Ibid

Huron such as the little thriving port town of Alcona. Typically, the *Marine City* would travel to specific villages and towns along the coast of Michigan between Detroit and Mackinac and back again. Advertisements in newspapers of that time announced that the *Marine City* would leave Ward's Dock in Detroit every Monday at midnight and would stop at the towns and villages of Forestville, Au Sable, Harrisville, Alcona, Alpena, Crawford's Quarry, Duncan and Mackinac, "all intermediate lake shore ports." Fare for a round trip was $12.[6]

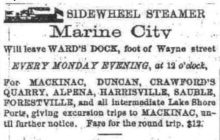

One article in the August 13, 1869 Port Huron Times said the "Steamer *MARINE CITY* passed up on Tuesday on her way to Mackinac with a large number of excursionists on board accompanied by the Pontiac Band, which sports splendid music. As usual, she was gaily decorated with flags."

In 1875, her first year of round trip regular passenger service, the *Marine City* was southbound when she encountered very

---

[6] Advertisements in Detroit Adv., June 28, 1870

rough waters off Sturgeon Point in Lake Huron. The heavy sea "stove in her side and carried away her hall stairway, and the rush of water into her being so great it was with great difficulty that she was righted and relieved, and taken into the port of Au Sable for repairs..."[7] Five years later the *Marine City* would suffer a far greater tragedy, as the town of Alcona would bear witness.

PORT OF CALL
THE TOWN OF ALCONA
In 1880's

For four decades, the town of Alcona was the only adequately sheltered port of entry between Alpena and Bay City that had heavy off-loading docking capabilities. The town also boasted a narrow gauge railroad that ran out onto the main pier. Alcona, known early on as "The Cove," was nestled on the western shore of Lake Huron between Sturgeon Point and another promontory point to the north known as Alcona Pointe. It was a small, but bustling port providing safe harbor from all but direct easterly winds. Solid rock and wood cairns supported its long pier that extended out 326 feet, providing further protection (See Plat Map, figure 1, page 73)

---

[7] Toronto Daily Globe, 10/23/1875

Alcona was originally a simple place with humble beginnings. A man calling himself Commodore William Hill from Lockport, New York, ventured to the Alcona area by boat on May 15th, 1845 and established a fishery in the natural protective cove near the rich fishing grounds of northern Lake Huron, where lake sturgeon, herring, whitefish and perch were plentiful. Abundant quantities of fish thrived in close right off the shore. During the 1850's and later on through the Civil War, one could see nets extending from the shoreline out to buoys in a straight line which were ranged from range markers at the shoreline points. Fish were caught, cleaned, salted and packed in barrels made from the great white pines and shipped on schooners and later on steamers such as the Marine City. Fishing shanties dotted the coast between High Banks (Springport south of Harrisville) and Black River. In 1867 fishing employed sixty men in Harrisville, south of Alcona, using four sailboats and four trap net skiffs with a yearly catch from Harrisville alone of 5,000 barrels for a gross revenue of $40,000.00.[8] The town of Alcona was established with the advent of its first commercial enterprise. In years to come, Commodore Hill expanded his modest trade to include several fishing boats and

---

[8] Sterline, Elrita M. *First Fifty Years of Harrisville.* Central Michigan University, 1967; Clarke Historical Library, Mount Pleasant, Michigan. $40.000.00 dollars is roughly equivalent to $531,516.63 in 2006 using inflation calculator at www.westegg.com/inflation

tugboats. He later married Lydia Horton, who died in Alcona on December 28, 1875. She had been married to Commodore Hill in 1857. After her death the Commodore could be seen riding his "colossal sulky" at high speeds down the sawdust lane from Alcona all the way to Harrisville. His wife would never have let him drive the sulky so fast.[9] Hill built Alcona's first hotel and general store as well. He personally directed the rescue of three different ships saving passengers and freight on Lake Huron. Those three ships were 1) the *Benjamin Franklin* which ran aground on Thunder Bay Island saving its passengers; 2) a U.S. Revenue Cutter where he saved the crew; 3) the *Marine City* where his two fishing row boats manned by his sons Barney and Samuel and his workmen Jim Johnson and Charles Flick saved many of the passengers and crew of the *Marine City*. Commodore Hill died March 30, 1894 and is buried at Mt. Joy Cemetery up the hill from the ghost town of Alcona next to his wife Lydia.[10]

Alcona had the reputation of being a healthy place with good clean water and air, yet the Commodore's wife died relatively young of an unknown condition. Tuberculosis, cholera, smallpox, dysentery, flu and

---

[9] Schelley, Marie. *Alcona, a Ghost Town.* Central Michigan University, 1967; Clark Historical Library, Mt. Pleasant, Michigan.
[10] Schelley, Marie. *Alcona, a Ghost Town.* Central Michigan University, 1967; Clark Historical Library, Mt. Pleasant, Michigan.

infections easily contracted by poor dental hygiene and marginal sewage practices claimed many people in their prime.[11] Intentional, violent deaths were rare with 200 reported homicides in all of the United States in 1880.[12]

Many of those who made Michigan their home were originally from New England and western New York. The trip west became easier once the Erie Canal opened up in 1825.

New England was the center of abolitionist sentiment, and immigrants from there brought their sentiments with them to Michigan. So, prior to the Civil War, Michigan citizens in small towns such as Alcona played an active role in opposing slavery. Michigan towns were often the final stop in the United States for the Underground Railroad for fugitive slaves trying to get north and find work in friendly towns along the way.[13]

Johnson, Haynes and Company was the town of Alcona's first lumber company in 1865 after the Civil War ended.[14] That same year a newly formed lumber corporation known as

---

[11] A leading cause of death in the U.S. was diarrhea in 1880.

[12] This figure does not include known deaths in the Reconstruction Period following the Civil War, including lynchings in the south and often unreported outlaw violence out west. It also does not include religious massacres allegedly involving the Mormons.

[13] The Republican Party was founded in Jackson, Michigan in 1854 to oppose the extension of slavery northward. From 1854 until 1932, Michigan usually voted for Republican candidates. During this period the entire electoral vote of the state was not once given to a Democratic presidential candidate. http://encarta.msn.com/text_76157168_45/Michigan.html

[14] Schelley, Marie. *Alcona, a Ghost Town.* Central Michigan University, 1967; Clark Historical Library, Mt. Pleasant, Michigan.

the Alger Smith and Company, owned by Russell Alger and Martin S. Smith, bought most of the land along the Lake Huron shoreline near Alcona.[15] Extensive lumbering followed for well over three decades. During a "winter without snow" in 1878, Alcona lumbermen took out 3,000,000 board feet of lumber and navigation was open all year on Lake Huron.[16] This greedy, highly successful venture would eventually be the undoing of Alcona. However, it fueled and financed the political aspirations of the head of Alcona's Alger Smith and Company, Russell A. Alger, who became the Republican Governor of Michigan in 1885 and then later ran unsuccessfully for the presidency of the United States after becoming Alcona's first millionaire. [17] He served as Secretary of War during the Spanish

---

[15] In the 1870s, Smith transferred his share of the sawmill operations in Alcona to James Beard. Russell Alger later sold his interest in the sawmill to Agnes Beard, James Beard's wife, for $25,000. A year later, she sold her share for $30,000, making $5,000, a fortune in those days, in a year. (Note: There were no capital gains taxes at that time.)

[16] The lumbering business was established in 1865 in Alcona Township by the firm of Johnson, Haynes & Company, consisting of John Johnston, Elijah Haynes, James Beard, F.H. Vandenburg. All were originally from Port Huron, MI. See Historical Background of Alcona County, from Historical Facts and Stories You Should Know About Alcona County, compiled by Neelie Hansen, The Northern Journal, Volume IV, Issue I, Winter 2006, page 33 also The Northern Journal, Spring 2006, Volume IV, Issue II.

[17] "The Alger Company was one of the largest producers of pine timber, spars and masts in the world, and of excellent quality. It had 25 miles of railroad, 3 ½ feet gauge, laid with steel rails, and four locomotives of which the General Sheridan weighed 64,000 pounds." Historical Background of Alcona County, from Historical Facts and Stories You Should Know About Alcona County, compiled by Neelie Hansen, The Northern Journal, Volume IV, Issue I, Winter 2006, page 33.

American War under William McKinley.[18]

    Russell Alger's story, which began in 1836, is a testament to determination and perseverance. He was the son of a failed farmer in Ohio. At 12 years of age, both of his parents died, and he was left trying to assume responsibility for his three siblings. That challenge was just too great for a child of 12, and the children were separated, each going to live with a relative.[19]

    The young man worked hard as a laborer on a farm. The money that he earned was spent on schooling with what was left over going to his sisters. He had hoped to attend college but did not have the money. He did teach school for a couple of years and then "read the law" under the supervision of two lawyers in Akron, Ohio. He passed his examination for the bar but did not stay long in the legal profession. He wanted to work at something more physically challenging, less tedious and preferably outdoors. So, he went to Michigan.[20]

    Along with a partner, Alger founded a shingle mill in Grand Rapids in 1860. At first, he did well. However, the Civil War and changing political climate changed that. In 1861, the lumber market collapsed. So did the shingle mill, and Alger lost everything and

---

[18] *Deep Woods Frontier, A History of Logging in Northern Michigan,*
Theodore J. Karamanski, Wayne Sate University Press, Detroit, MI 1989, p.57
[19] Ibid
[20] Ibid

went to work as a wood sawer to pay off the creditors. With the Civil War raging, he decided to prove himself once more and raised a company of cavalry and was appointed a captain in the Michigan Guard. He fought in many of the most horrible battles of the war, including Gettysburg and assembled an admirable service record. At the end of the war, he was commissioned a brevet brigadier general. During this time he made some important friendships with Generals George Armstrong Custer and Philip Sheridan. He also made the acquaintance of Abraham Lincoln. [21]

In late 1864, Alger returned from the war and moved his family to Detroit. He became involved in a variety of business ventures including investments in oil lands, saw mills and a brick company. The brick company failed, but Alger acquired control over several barges and a schooner. Within six months, he had made a small fortune in a new enterprise of shipping lumber on the lakes. Once again he was part of the lumber business. In northern Michigan, he bought government timberland for usually no more than $1.25 an acre. He had learned to be a careful businessman and that led to more success. He was also willing to embrace innovations and became one of the first lumbermen in Michigan to build a railroad to

---

[21] Ibid, pp. 56-57

transport his lumber in Alcona.[22] In spring of 1878, Russell A. Alger and Company of Detroit completed 13 miles of railroad in Alcona County. This railroad utilized three locomotives and 51 cars. There were three other logging railroads that were constructed out of Greenbush at the time as well.[23]

Alger also bought land in the Upper Peninsula of Michigan, having the foresight to realize well in advance that he was rapidly depleting the lumber resources of the Lower Peninsula of Michigan.[24]

Alger truly was a self-made lumber king. He specialized in cutting giant pine and cedar for spars and masts. Alger and his partners controlled more than 50,000 acres of forest lands in Alcona and Alpena Counties. His bases were located in Harrisville, Black River and Alcona, Michigan on the shores of Lake Huron. Their annual cut rate in 1881 exceeded more than 60 million board feet, a rate which would quickly deplete the resources available to them.

Like many candidates, Russell Alger wanted to appear as a friend of the working man as he campaigned for political office and gorged himself on a non-renewable resource. During the campaign for governor, he observed some of his lumberjacks driving logs

---

[22] Ibid, page 57

[23] www.michiganrailroads.com/RRHX/timeline/1870s/timeline1870s.htm

[24] *Deep Woods Frontier, A History of Logging in Northern Michigan*, Theodore J. Karamanski, Wayne State University Press, Detroit, MI 1989, p. 57

in very cold water on a bitterly cold spring morning in northern Lake Huron. Within earshot of a reporter, he asked them how much they were paid and he was told "A $1.75 a day and chuck when we are near enough to the wanigan to eat." This seemingly surprised Alger, and he told the foreman "That's not enough for such work. Raise them." The pay was immediately raised by the foreman, but after Alger departed, it was again cut back, the foreman being familiar with the routine. Ironically, it was a former section hand on one of Alger's companies who assassinated President McKinley in 1901.[25]

By that year, the forests of Lower Michigan had been greatly exploited and the Alger Smith and Company was turning its gaze elsewhere. The depletion of the forests of Michigan was not a great concern to Alger. He figured that if he did not cut the pine, someone else would, and there was a need for cleared land to farm. The logging had reduced the forests to slashings which easily caught fire. The fires ruined the soil and hurt the future of the area even more.[26]

Some have claimed that more millionaires were made in the years 1860-1890 from unrestrained, non-sustainable lumbering than in any other era in American history, including the computer era of 1990s. In these

---

[25] Ibid, page 58
[26] Ibid, pp 58-59.

years there was no income tax, no capital gains tax and very little property tax. It was much easier to accumulate and hold vast amounts of wealth during these unregulated, exploitive times.

Trust accounts, many surviving now in Monaco today, set up during this period are still viable today paying out to beneficiaries more than 130 years later.[27] Trust experts noted that these payments are still "spoiling children for generations to come from the slash and burn ruination of northern Michigan's lumbering era."[28] Many of Michigan's older villages and cities still have Lumber Baron Mansions dating to this era. One such mansion was Alger's summer house located north of Alcona in Black River which was used regularly by his Superintendent J. Millen in his absence. (Figure 2, p. 74-75)

The lumber industry in Michigan began around 1840 when the great demand for lumber outpaced the traditional sources of white pine in Maine and New York. Michigan was the next state west, strategically located in the climatic northern pine belt latitudes

---

[27] Hon. J. Russell Huges, Probate Judge of Alcona County

[28] Michigan lumber barons netted $4 billion dollars during the period from 1848 to 1898. That was about $93,437,109,439.31 in 2006 (using currency converter found at www.westegg.com/inflation). That is a billion dollars more than came out of the state of California during the Gold Rush of that same time period. 19.5 million acres of Michigan forest were stripped. Virtually none of it was replanted. The worthless land was abandoned by the lumber barons, who ignored the tax bills on the barren land, and reverted back to state ownership (http://info.detnews.com/history/story/index.dfm?id=90&category=governme nt)

with its towering virgin white pines. Lumbering in Michigan, though, quickly surpassed the scope of previous lumbering endeavors and became the most important industry in the state.[29]

Between 1840 and 1860, the Saginaw Valley was the leading lumbering area. During this period the number of mills operating in the state doubled. In addition to the increase in the number of mills, the value of the products saw an increase from $1 million dollars to $6 million dollars annually. By 1869, the Saginaw Valley alone was earning $7 million dollars per year, a vast sum in those days.[30] Cash was king indeed, and as lumbering moved north with the need for more giant white pine, remote Northern ports, like Alcona of Michigan, became economic bonanzas where it was easier to access and ship out the lumber.[31]

The United States became a large exporter of wood products from 1870 to 1900 largely because of northern Michigan. Between the years 1870 and 1879 the earnings averaged about 18 million dollars a year from

---

[29] Lumbering in Michigan, Maria Quinlan, www.michigan.gov

[30] $7 million dollars is roughly equal to $102,309,175.59 in 2006 (using inflation calculator found at : (www.westegg.com/inflation). Interestingly, Canada passed a law barring the entry of "poor people" for any reason during these times. Ibid.

[31] When the pioneers first settled Michigan's interior during the 1830s most of the land was covered in trees. It was said that a squirrel could travel across the entire state of Michigan from tree branch to tree branch without ever touching the ground. "Introducing Michigan's Past" Michigan History Magazine, an overview for teachers. Copyright Michigan Department of State, 2001.

northern Michigan alone.   It peaked at $21,353,721.00 in 1874. [32]

"Big Wheels" originally ran over the tops of downed cut timber and the logs would be chained up to clear the ground. Then a horse would pull them out of the forest to an area for milling or rafting on Lake Huron.[33] Many rivers, such as the Muskegon, the AuSable, the Thunder Bay River, the Pere Marquette River, the Black River, the Grand River and the Tittabawasee River became important means of transporting logs. Logging, however, destroyed the pebble fish breeding beds of these rivers, including the fish spawning beds coming up from the Great Lakes.[34]

Rafting, which consisted of strong chains strung through holes drilled in each log's end attached to outside booms was a common way of transporting logs to market on the Great Lakes. The booms set up a large secure perimeter which was done in very calm water called a crib. In 1880, the cost of the chains alone to set up such a raft was approximately $15,000. ($15,000 is roughly equivalent to $313,159.75 in 2006, from www.westegg.com) Specially trained horses

[32] Bay City "The Evening Press"
$21,353,721.00 is roughly equal to $346,909,765.11 in 2006. (Using inflation calculator – www.westegg.com/inflation.
[33] Schelley, Marie. *Alcona, a Ghost Town.* Central Michigan University, 1967; Clarke Historical Library, Mount Pleasant, Michigan.
[34] Alexander, Jeff. *The Muskegon.* Michigan State University Press, East Lansing, MI, 2006.

had to swim out into Lake Huron with a rider on them pulling long timber chains together for booms. The *Vulcan* on one occasion took 2,400,000 feet of timber to Cleveland in a raft from Alcona and Black River.[35]

For 30 years, starting in 1869, Michigan produced more lumber than any other state. As production increased, the loggers moved away from the rivers and penetrated the interiors of both the upper and lower peninsulas using narrow gauge railroads. Alcona and Black River eventually had interconnecting railroads and were key ports.

Alcona owed its vibrant existence to the fact that it was the seat of extensive lumbering firms, such as James Beard and Company and the Alger Smith and Company, as well as its protective cove and substantial pier on Lake Huron. The James Beard Company in Alcona had a large saw mill, a lath mill, a shingle mill. It was supplied with lumber by a railroad that ran on a three feet six inch gauge and was 12 miles in length.[36] In 1877, the mill employed 30 men and cut 3,000,000 feet of logs.[37] In 1878, Beard and Co. built a ten mile long private logging road that ran from Alcona to the west into the

---

[35] Sterling, Elrita M. *First Fifty Years of Harrisville.* Central Michigan University, 1967; Clarke Historical Library, Mount Pleasant, Michigan.
[36] Alcona County Review, September 10. 1880, Volume 4, No. 21.
[37] Schelley, Marie. *Alcona, a Ghost Town.* Central Michigan University, 1967; Clark Historical Library, Mt. Pleasant, Michigan.

interior. [38] The first railroad tracks emanating out of Alcona to pick up inland timber were made out of maple wood with motive power by horses. Later steel tracks were laid with steam engines providing the pulling power supplied by Russell Alger's Company. [39]

Because of demand over the years, the white pine harvested later was younger and inferior in size. By 1889, the year of greatest lumber production, Michigan produced about 5.5 million board feet but was decimating its forests and land. [40]

Lumber camps or lumber barracks operated round the clock, but with a 6-day work week. They were at full capacity generally in the winter with a roaring fire centrally located inside that kept them cozy. The workers generally started work two hours before sunrise and did not return to the camp until sunset. Men generally bet in the morning who could accomplish the most work during the day. The only time of rest was after supper and before bedtime. The men also did not work on Sundays and "gillen" days. Gillen days occurred when the weather was too stormy to work. Men loved gillen days, as they generally still received a portion of their pay. Saturday night was spent singing

---

[38] www.michiganrailroads.com/RRHX/timeline/1870s/timeline1870sbackup.ht
m
[39] Schelley, Marie. *Alcona, a Ghost Town*. Central Michigan University, 1967; Clark Historical Library, Mt. Pleasant, Michigan.
[40] Lumbering in Michigan, Maria Quilan, www.michigan.gov.

songs, dancing, playing games, especially checkers and card games and playing jokes on new arrivals to camp. Almost every barrack had an accordion and a violin player. They were considered comfortable and warm in the winter, sleeping up to 100 men. Mattresses were made of straw and there was always a central chair for weekly barbering of the men.[41]

The food at the typical lumber camp in Alcona was good and plentiful. Meals consisted of salt pork, beans, corned beef, dried apple pies, tea, coffee, bread, potatoes, cake, cookies, and butter. If a stranger was present, he was served at no charge.[42]

Every lumber camp had a "scaler" who was usually the best educated of the group. He settled all arguments and helped the men write letters home and do their "figuring."[43]

During the 1880s and 1890s, the lumber companies sold large tracts of land that had already been logged for farmland. To sell it they advertised the land as good farmland, ready to be plowed. That was not true as large troublesome stumps had to be removed, and the fertility of the land was quickly exhausted. Families that bought the land often had to give it up when it did not

---

[41] Schelley, Marie. *Alcona, a Ghost Town*. Central Michigan University, 1967; Clarke Historical Library, Mount Pleasant, Michigan.
[42] Ibid
[43] Ibid

produce enough to pay the property taxes, small as they were. The State of Michigan acquired this tax delinquent land as well as land that was simply abandoned by some lumber companies and farmers. This land formed the basis for the state's early but inadequate efforts toward reforestation and land management.[44] Land sold for as little as $1 to $5 an acre in the Alcona area.[45] The greedy lumber barons were followed by a state government greedy for tax revenue and land tax sales which generated state sponsored land speculation attracting unsuspecting and uninformed new foreign arrivals to Michigan.

Prior to logging, wild rice abounded everywhere.[46] Wild rice is native only to North America. It is a five-foot-tall aquatic plant that has, in addition to being a staple food, played an important role in the culture and religious ceremonies of the Chippewa.[47] In addition to the toll lumbering took on the fertility of the land, the extensive lumbering activities destroyed wild rice along the rivers and caused forest fires. Tree cutting left short second undergrowth and dry, dead treetops from large great white tine trees. This

---

[44] Lumbering in Michigan, Maria Quilan, www.michigan.gov.
[45] From an advertisement appearing in the Alcona County Review from JAS Beard and Company "good lands for sale in Alcona County from $1.00 to $5.00 per acre."
[46] Alexander, Jeff. *The Muskegon.* Michigan State University Press, East Lansing, MI, 2006.
[47] *Restoring a Lost Legacy*, Doreen Cubie, *National Wildlife,* June/July, 2007, p.39.

created ideal kindling for forest fires which would rage so intensely that they actually interfered with navigation when the westerly prevailing smoke moved across Lake Huron creating "fog like" conditions.[48]

On July 11, 1911 one lumber town 17 miles south of Alcona, Oscoda, Michigan, burned to the ground. Oscoda was a typical lumbering town with a surplus of bark from the mills. This bark was often spread on the streets to prevent mud-like conditions and ruts. Oscoda was a lakeside town and didn't have cement or gravel to surface its streets. While the bark provided some firmness and a ground cover, it also made it the ideal kindling for the fire. When the Oscoda fire raged, Jennie Kulber, a resident of Oscoda, tells of reaching Lake Huron safely to find a crowd of people, dogs, chickens and other animals in the water. Some people had wet blankets that they used to cover themselves and sometimes shared with others who had no protection.

Lumbering in the latter part of the 19th Century brought millions of dollars into Michigan. The money went mostly to the lumber barons, then the lumbermen, the people who worked to supply them and to the state in property taxes. Lumbermen in 1880 earned about $25 monthly working long hours in the woods. An average monthly wage in

---

[48] *Shingle Shavers and Berry Pickers,* Oliver Raymond.

other occupations was about $10 per month. Lumbermill hands earned upwards of $35 monthly.[49]

The inevitable decline of lumbering had a devastating impact on the State of Michigan and its communities. Individuals and the economies of entire villages, such as Alcona, collapsed. Lumbered lands were largely unable to offer profitable farming operations and a revenue stream to pay taxes, so the Michigan economy collapsed.[50]

The decline of Alcona started in 1886, but Alcona was still producing the following that year: 1) 485 cords of Hemlock bark at $4.00 per cord; 2) 785,000 Pine and Hemlock lumber; 3) 9,925 Cedar posts; 4) 4,000 Cedar ties; 5) 608,000 Cedar shingles; 6) 15,000 lbs of barreled salted fish.[51]

As the decline started, imagine those sand, sawdust and bark covered streets, the plank sidewalks with their numerous patches; aged and unattractive framed school houses, broken down mills, and men with their families who now had to move away for lack of work. After the closing of the mills there were scores of empty houses with windows gone and doors broken in. In some areas, when the big mills closed or burned down, the

---

[49] *Shingle Shavers and Berry Pickers,* "Oliver Raymond.

[50] Lumbering in Michigan, Maria Quinlan, www.michigan.gov.

[51] Schelley, Marie. *Alcona, a Ghost Town.* Central Michigan University, 1967; Clarke Historical Library, Mount Pleasant, Michigan; $4.00 in 1886 is approximately equivalent to $86.56 in 2006. (Calculated using the inflation calculator at www.westegg.com/inflation)

houses were taken apart, loaded on railroad cars and moved away or loaded on sleds and moved inland during the winter to area farms.[52]

But in the heyday of lumbering, the people inhabiting the town of Alcona who were not out cutting and hauling trees to port, generally worked in well compensated service oriented trades. In fact, there was zero unemployment in lumbering towns from circa 1850 until 1893.[53] Most had their own well-defined skill and place, usually based on providing a much needed service. One simply had to be useful in some way to survive. There was no government welfare system, and sparse charity was dispensed only by local churches, often with heavy doses of religious dogma.

During its rapid growth and at the height of its prosperity the town of Alcona had a succession of general stores, a railroad depot, a passenger and freight dock complete with railroad tracks to its end, three hotels, one of which was a three-story building. Alcona was platted with the State of Michigan in August 1880. It had an established year-round population according to the official U.S.

---

[52] The Northern Journal, Spring 2006, Volume IV, Issue II

[53] Sterline, Elrita M. *First Fifty Years of Harrisville.* Central Michigan University, 1967; Clarke Historical Library, Mount Pleasant, Michigan.

Census[54] with large numbers of transient workers in the surrounding forests. There were two express stations, one run by American and the other by McClure's; a Western Union Telegraph office; a post office. The Postmaster was E.R. Haynes. Alcona was on a railroad spur serving the J L & S R Railroad line circa 1885 (later known as the Detroit and Mackinac line) with its own railroad station by 1885. Passenger service along the northeast coast of Michigan was suspended in 1951, but freight railroad service continues to run to this day. In 1879, Harrisville, Alcona and Black River started stringing telephone lines located between homes in Harrisville, originally; and then between the town's homes. The telephone did not extend outside the area and telegraph was still the only outside contact along with the mail.[55]

One of the hotels in Alcona, "The Rookery," was three stories high. Another hotel was known as the Union Hotel. The Alcona House, another hotel, advertised "first class accommodations for traveling public. Good barn and general store in connection with hotel." For $12.00 per month one could obtain room and board consisting of food,

[54] In 1886, Alcona was a town that fluctuated between 1,000 to 1,400 residents. Schelley, Marie. *Alcona, a Ghost Town*. Central Michigan University, 1967; Clarke Historical Library, Mount Pleasant, Michigan
[55] Sterline, Elrita M. *First Fifty Years of Harrisville*, Central Michigan University, 1967; Clark Historical Library, Mount Pleasant, Michigan.

lodging and tobacco. You were charged for the tobacco even if you did not use it.[56]

Business directories from 1875-1885 listed the following establishments: a lumber dealer by the name of Alger R.A. and Company; a lumber company, The Alger Smith and Company; Backus and Brothers General Store; Carl Fred Hotel and Planing Mill; Carl WF General Store; William Farrand, Fisherman; Thomas Gullifer and Sons Saw Mill; E.R. Haynes Saw Mill and Express Agent; William Hill Fisherman; Ives Green and Company Saw Mill; George J. Johnson Hotel; Coopersmith owned by Henry Jones; a lumber dealer run by N. McNally; and C.E. Smith General Store. Alcona also had Methodist, Episcopalian and Presbyterian Churches and what was considered a "good district school." It also had a stagecoach that ran daily to Harrisville. The principle industries included lumber, shingles, fish, and cordwood. The nearest bank was in Alpena. J.O. Dayton was a Justice of the Peace. The two full-time town doctors were Dr. H. Herring and Dr. J.H. Stockwell. (Stockwell was later saved in the *Marine City* disaster.) There was also a Blacksmith by the name of Charles Lawson. McGuire ran a saloon and hotel in Alcona. James Moore was a harness maker. His successor was Newt Edwards, who was later written up in the Guinness Book of Records

---

[56] Schelley, Marie. *Alcona, a Ghost Town*. Central Michigan University, 1967; Clarke Historical Library, Mount Pleasant, Michigan

when he became mayor of Alcona and later still the only Mayor of a ghost town (see figure 8, page 85). Isaac Mosser was a carpenter. Packard and Company was a Fishery. James Beard and Company was a lumber manufacturer and express agent. George Bryant and Company ran a general store and drug store. Henry Cunningham ran a hotel. William Clark also ran a general store. Ed Dennis succeeded the first Justice of the Peace, Judge Dayton. The Teacher was L. Frederick. Another hotel was run by William Lumhard. The livestock dealer was Joseph Miller. Thomas Miller ran a general store. William Milligan was a carpenter. A resident George S. Ritchie was a thresher.

The Post Office in Alcona was established January 9, 1867 and ran until the August 15, 1903.

The people of Alcona had family lineages from Prussia, Canada, Kentucky, New York, Ireland, France, Norway, Sweden, England, Scotland, Maine, Illinois, New Brunswick, Nova Scotia, Massachusetts, New Hampshire, New Jersey and one from Brazil. Skills listed in an 1870 census for Alcona included "keeps boardinghouse," domestic servant, works shingle mill, works saw mill, breakman, fireman, teamster, blacksmith, laborer in saw mill, car greaser, bookkeeper, night watchman in mill, chore boy, house carpenter, keeping house, filer in saw mill, rafts man, farmer, laborer, lumberman, fisherman, saloon keeper, hotel keeper, mill engineer, locomotive engineer, shoe maker, butcher, photographer, artist, physician, lawyer.

The average age of the residents was early to mid-20s, but there were several residents in their 60s, a few in their 70s and at least one in her 90s (ninety-three to be exact). Only 20 out of 400 who responded to the census claimed they could not read or write. Over a dozen homes had private domestic servants.

HOUSING

The early basic houses in Alcona were built of logs and measured 14' x 16' with walls approximately 5'6'' in height. It took about six weeks to build a primitive log cabin, without a door, a floor, a chimney or anything else besides the logs and roof. The roof was covered with strips of bark and a few scattered boards made up the floor. There was really no means of getting boards for a floor early on. The only alternative was to use an axe to split slabs of oak for the floor. For some cabins, the roofing would consist of logs hollowed out like a trough and laid side-by-side with their edges close together and the trough side up. Then, there would be another row which was reversed and covered the edges of the first laid row.[57]

Consider the following account of one Northern Michigan pioneer:

> I was most anxious for a door, as the wolves would come about in the evening and some times stay all night and keep up a serenade that almost chill the blood in my veins. Of all the noises I think the howling of wolves and the yell of Indians the most fearful; at least it appeared so to me then when I was not able to close the door against them. I had the greatest terror of Indians; for I had never seen any before I came to Michigan. I had seen Oneidas, but they were different, being partially civilized.[58]

The cabin might have an ordinary stick and round chimney or a type of box made of split logs that was located at one end of the room. The box would be filled with dirt and ashes, and a fire would be built in the center of it. There would be an opening cut into the roof that allowed smoke to exit the house, although that wasn't always efficient and smoke would float around the cabin. The log homes, if made well with a door, were easy to keep clean, though, and they were cool in the summer and warm in the winter. The color of

---

[57] *Birchbark Belles, Women on the Michigan Frontier,* edited by Larry B. Massie, The Priscilla Press, Allegan Forest, Michigan, 1993.
[58] Ibid

the logs fit in well with the soil and surrounding vegetation. The bark that was left on and the neatly sawn off corners made the cabins picturesque.[59]

During this period, the barter system was very active in the upper Great Lakes and involved the trading of animal hides, tanning bark, shingles, posts, barrels[60], barrel staves made of ash, and the like. Salt pork, bacon, salt, fish, flour, meal, molasses, dried apples, tobacco, boots, bolts of cloth, gun powder, axes and saws were very common trade items that were carried on steamers such as the *Marine City*. As far as actual prices go[61], in 1869 a pair of boots routinely cost $7, and a pair of shoes cost $1.50 a pair. At that time cedar shingles were valued at $1.50 per thousand. Sheaves of cedar shingles were widely used as legal tender in bartering and trading transactions to obtain supplies off steamers.[62]

The natural richness of the wild land in northern Michigan provided much of the diet for the early settlers. The prairie

---

[59] *Birchbark Bells, Women on the Michigan Frontier*, edited by Larry B. Massie, The Priscilla Press, Allegan Forest, Michigan, 1993.

[60] In the 1850s the long, large Great White Pines were ideal for barrel making which became a big industry along the northeast shoreline of Michigan on Lake Huron.

Sterline, Elrita M. *First Fifty Years of Harrisville.* Central Michigan University, 1967; Clarke Historical Library, Mount Pleasant, Michigan.

[61] Other interesting facts from 1880 include:

    The U.S. average wage was 15 cents an hour in the U.S.

    Sugar was 3 cents a pound

    Eggs were 10 cents a dozen

    Coffee was 10 cents a pound

[62] *Shingle Shavers and Berry Pickers*, Oliver Raymond

strawberries were described as being large and sweet. The white fish of the Great Lakes was also a staple in the diet and was celebrated for its taste. Fish were plentiful and the extra were placed in half barrels and salted so that they would keep for future use or trade. Maple syrup, maple sugar and wild onions were also in plentiful supply. During the autumn, wild plums, crab apples and frost grapes were enjoyed. Honey was to be found in abundant supply in trees of Northern Michigan. Because of the honey, there was also beeswax for candles. In the 1800s, eggs were considered the best choice for diet while journeying through Michigan.[63]

Juneberries (sometimes known as serviceberries) and huckleberries were also a major food source at this time. Other food items that might be found in a well stocked cellar in the autumn, would have included a bin of potatoes, heads of cabbage, a crock or two of Sauerkraut, another of salt-brine cucumbers, and packed in boxes of sand, red beets, carrots and turnips. The shelves would be full of canned fruit, mostly wild berries, tomatoes and pickles of many kinds. Pickled cucumbers, red beets, waxed beans, green tomatoes, corn relish, chow-chow (while there are variations, chow-chow is a "crunchy, sweet-and-sour combination of

---

[63] *Birchbark Bells, Women on the Michigan Frontier,* edited by Larry B. Massie, The Priscilla Press, Allegan Forest, Michigan 1993.

cabbage, carrots and green bell pepper."[64]),
mixed pickles and more would be canned. [65]

During the winter, corn meal mush was
an item often eaten. Navy beans were a
staple, cooked with hambone and added to
soups. Quite often, something sour was
served with meals and was considered a
delicacy. [66]

The summer weather, of course, had a
lot to do with how well stocked the cellars
were for the winter. Winters in Michigan
could be hard, and by the time spring arrived,
the jars that had been full were empty and
any vegetables left in sand would be wrinkled
and tasteless. The dried corn and beans would
be gone and everybody would be hungry for
something fresh. One might dig up the first
parsnips as soon as the frost was out of the
ground, and they were considered a
wonderful treat. Other spring treats included
winter onion and white onions in dandelion
gravy. By mid-May there would be morel
mushrooms, another tasty treat. Gardens
would be planted, usually with asparagus and
rhubarb beds established in them. [67] Yet it
would be the arrival of a ship that brought the
greatest promise after the ice broke on the
Great Lakes, usually in early April.

---

[64] Pioneer Thinking, www.pioneerthinking.com/aicr_chowchowrelish.html
[65] The Northern Journal, Spring 2006, Volume IV, Issue II
[66] Ibid.
[67] Ibid.

The summer months of June, July and August were the time for berry picking, starting with Juneberries and raspberries, then blueberries, and, finally, blackberries into August. Summer suppers might consist of bread, milk and berries. During the summer months food items were kept cool by using well water that was pumped through a wooden chest, keeping the temperature cool.[68]

Despite the presence of numerous sources of food, cooking could still be a challenge. Matches were not readily available[69] and it was often necessary for a family member to visit a neighbor's house located miles away and bring back something called a fire brand, a glowing end of a charcoal-like burning stick. It had to be swung to keep it burning during a long walk back.[70]

---

[68] Ibid.

[69] The Diamond Match Company patented the first nonpoisonous match in the United States in 1910. President William H. Taft publicly asked them to release their patent for the "good of mankind." They did so on January 28, 1911. http://inventors.about.com/library/inventors/blmatch.htm.

[70] The Northern Journal, Spring 2006, Volume IV, Issue II.

MEDICINE

It was said that the early medical practitioners were often more deadly than the diseases that they were attempting to treat.[71] These pioneer doctors definitely faced different challenges than doctors face today with far fewer effective methods of treatment.

This account from a northern Michigan pioneer describes the challenges faced by both doctor and patient.

> A doctor at last came to settle in our village. Doctor Sumner was tall and nice and very dignified. He would enter a house, hear the patient's story of shaking and suffering in perfect silence. Then he would say, "Yes I see you all run down, very weak, bilious, debilitated. We must draw off all the bad blood and give you a chance to make new and get strong again, give me a bowl and a bandage." All would be bled for a charge of a dollar and fifty cents extra for bleeding. The doctor forgot his lance one day and took out a jack knife and sharpened it on his boot and bled all the family. When he came to little Susan the hurt and fright was so great that she died in his arms. He came to our house, but mother would not let him touch any of the children. Father was growing worse and tried the Doctor's remedy.

---

[71] *Birchbark Belles, Women on the Michigan Frontier*

In fifteen minutes he was dead. Another doctor who came said "that was no way to do," he never bled his patients, he wound them in a wet sheet. A promising young man, one of the very best, Sumner Hammlund, was wrapped in cold wet sheets but soon got the chill and died. Yet another Doctor came and he sent a man and a team down to Grand Ledge to get a load of hemlock bark which he would seep strong tea and give them hemlock sweats when they were so weak that they died from the heat and exhaustion. You may ask did these doctors get rich. Oh no, they got the shakes, took some of their own medicines and soon died.[72](sic)

Small town doctors of the late 1800s often owned their own small drugstores. They would grow herbs as potted plants in their offices. The plants and seeds were used to make a variety of herbal drugs which were used to help treat the common cold, stomach aches, kidney ailments and the ague (swamp fever). The potted herbs could grow to be four to six feet tall.[73] Natural remedies were used for a variety of ailments. In an account by Arthur Scott White detailing the early days around Alpena, a town about 30 miles north of Alcona, he speaks of gathering cranberries during the month of October in 1853 with

[72] Ibid
[73] The Way it Was, Remembering the Doctors Who Made House Calls, Al Eicher, The Lakeshore Guardian, www.lakeshoreguardian.com/_2004/072004/wayit_was.php

46

John W. Paxton, his stepfather and the captain of the schooner the Sparrow. He writes that "the cranberries so obtained proved of inestimable value to the little community at the mouth of the Devil River (Ossineke, Mich.) during the winter of 1854 in combating scurvy and intestinal disturbances."[74]

Life wasn't exactly easy for a small town doctor on the frontier. There were no real areas of specialty. The frontier doctor was surgeon, family practitioner, and obstetrician. Dr. Stockwell, an Alcona physician, held himself out also as a gynecologist.[75] Office hours left little time for house calls. Typical office hours were from 8 AM to 11 AM, 1 PM to 3 PM and 7 PM to 8 PM, and house calls were made at all hours – day or night. The doctor also had to be available for the outbreak of epidemics[76] such as typhoid fever and diphtheria.[77] Life expectancy, at the turn of the century, was

---

[74] Early Days Around Alpena, Arthur Scott White, Grand Rapids, Lansing Newspapers in Education, Inc. Provided by the *Lansing State Journal* and the Michigan Historical Center Foundation.
http://www.michigan.gov/documents/hal_mhc_mhm_schooner_tg_07-09-2002_92621_7.pdf
[75] From an advertisement appearing in the Alcona County Review in 1880, "G. Archie Stockwell, M.D. (late U.S. Navy) Surgeon and Gynecologist Alcona, Michigan. Office with J. Beard and Company."
[76] April 1, 1873, smallpox is said to have been stamped out in Alpena County. During the epidemic there had been over 1000 cases and 52 deaths in the county.
Alpena, Dates of Early Events, Part I, Compiled by John C. Viall, 1914, The Northern Journal, Volume IV, Issue I, Winter 2006, page 29.
[77] The Way it Was, Remembering the Doctors Who Made House Calls, Al Eicher, The Lakeshore Guardian,
www.lakeshoreguardian.com/_2004/072004/wayitwas.php.

only about 38.5 years of age in Northern Michigan.[78]

One disease that afflicted those living in Michigan was ague. There were numerous theories regarding how this disease became so common, from the cutting of trees to the concept that the disease was buried in the soil and released when the land was cleared or plowed. One theory stated that stagnant swamp water gave off a "miasma," or unhealthy air. None of these theories were correct, of course. It was, in fact, carried by Anopheles mosquitoes.[79] Significantly, Alcona had no incidences of ague afflictions as water was generally free flowing or came from very cold, non-stagnant springs.

The absence of the telephone provided another challenge for the doctor and the patient. Instead of placing a quick phone call, someone had to run out and find the doctor and bring the doctor to see the sick or injured patient. The patient might also be rushed to the doctor's home in the middle of

---

[78] "'The ways people described deaths a hundred years ago were very different from the terms we use today,' said Susan Hautaniemi Leonard, a researcher at the U of M Inter-University Consortium for Social and Political Research. 'But to understand why mortality rates have dropped, and what factors are critical in the spread of contagious diseases, we really need to know with a high degree of precision what people died from in the past. In the United States, the average life expectancy at birth has doubled since 1880, when the average life span was 38.5.'"
University of Michigan News Service, *Study Examines "Grammars of Death" to learn why we died*
http://www.ns.umich.edu/htdocs/releases/print.php?Releases/2004/Apr04/r04
2204
[79] *Birchbark Belles, Women on the Michigan Frontier*, edited by Larry B. Massie, The Priscilla Press, Allegan Forest, Michigan, 1993.

the night if an accident or illness required it.[80]

Milk sickness is perhaps one of the most mysterious ailments that afflicted the pioneers of the Midwest. It was unknown in Europe or any other continent except North America. By definition, milk sickness was caused by milk from cows that had eaten white snakeroot, a shade loving plant. This sickness has also been called puking fever, sick stomach, the slows, and the trembles and was most common in dry years when the cows wandered from the pastures to the woods in search of food and water. The symptoms experienced by humans included loss of appetite, listlessness, weakness, vague pains, muscle stiffness, vomiting, abdominal discomfort, severe constipation, bad breath and, finally, coma and death. Recovery from the sickness was slow and possibly never complete. More often than not, though, the attack was fatal.[81]

Dental care in the 1880s was also very different in Alcona than what we have today. At the end of the Civil War only three dental schools existed in the United States. Many of those practicing dentistry, such as barbers, blacksmiths and apothecarists, were

---

[80] The Way it Was, Remembering the Doctors Who Made House Calls, Al Eicher, The Lakeshore Guardian, www.lakeshoreguardian.com/_2004/072004/wayit was.php
[81] The Plant that Killed Nancy Hanks Lincoln, Lincoln Boyhood National Memorial.

"apprentice-trained itinerants."[82] At times, people received dental care from their physicians or they tried to take care of their dental needs themselves. They used such books as "The Family Physician and Guide to Health" which was published in 1833 in upstate New York, and was the bible for medical care through the turn of the century.[83] Tying a string around an infected tooth and yanking it out or using pliers in the hands of a friend or spouse were not uncommon treatments.

ENTERTAINMENT

The townspeople, in relatively remote locations, found ways of entertaining themselves. During the winter months, debating societies, singing schools and masquerade parties were forms of entertainment used to pass away the short days and long nights. Some winter nights would find large gatherings at one house of men, women and children. The gatherings would last all night and a large meal would be served at midnight. The time was spent singing and telling stories. Ghost stories were very popular at the time, as were war stories. There were still men living who had seen and met General George Washington and Anthony

---

[82] *A Short History of Modern Dentistry*, Edward Feinberg, DMD, http://www.wardny.com/history.html
[83] Ibid

Wayne and some who had fought in the War of 1812. Stories were told of Admiral Perry's heroes marching through western New York to reach the squadron that was being built on the shores of Lake Erie. Other stories included the tales of those who had fought at Tippecanoe or of those who had escaped the massacre at French Town[84]. The War of 1812 was referred to as "the late war."[85] It is interesting to note that after the War of 1812, veterans were rewarded with 120 acres of northern Michigan land. Much of the awarded acreage was near Alcona. However, many of the veterans simply sold out for cash right away without ever visiting their land; yet a large number of properties in the original chain of title still list the first veterans from the War of 1812.[86]

In the late 1870s and 1880s "jubilant dancing contests" were performed in the hotels and dance halls of Alcona. One of these contests involved the participants balancing a full glass of water upon their heads so that the "smoothest" dancing couple could be determined. A popular musician and orchestra leader, Joe Parrow, would

---

[84] The Battle of Frenchtown is also known as the River Raisin Massacre. It was an attempt by the Americans to retake Detroit during the War of 1812 and was a great defeat for the Americans. Frenchtown Charter Township is located south of Detroit. http://en.wikipedia.org/wiki/Battle_of_Frenchtown
[85] *Birchbark Belles, Women on the Michigan Frontier,* edited by Larry B. Massie, The Priscilla Press, Allegan Forest, Michigan, 1993.
[86] Sterling, Elrita M. *First Fifty Years of Harrisville.* Central Michigan University, 1967; Clarke Historical Library, Mount Pleasant, Michigan.

frequently play at Alcona's hotels[87]. Dancing was a favorite pastime and a good fiddler who could manage to stay sober and call dances was more in demand than a good doctor or preacher.[88] The patrons would feast on smoked lake sturgeon and fried fish eggs as a mainstay meal[89]. Even an annual Christmas Dance was held at one of the hotels or, occasionally, at a saloon. Celebrations on Memorial Day and on July 4th were also major events in the town.[90] It was a custom of the area from Harrisville to Alcona to Black River to celebrate the week after the 4th of July with dances every afternoon and evening.

---

[87] Alcona County Review, 1880s news accounts

[88] Sterling, Elrita M. *First Fifty Years of Harrisville.* Central Michigan University, 1967; Clarke Historical Library, Mount Pleasant, Michigan

[89] Another common dinner entrée during this time period was passenger pigeon. Passenger pigeon was served everywhere. At the time that the first white settlers made it to the Great Lakes region, the passenger pigeon very likely outnumbered any other bird species in the world. In the hardwoods of Michigan, Indiana and Ohio some of the nesting sites were three miles wide and thirty miles long. Such a site probably contained several million birds. The birds were loud and talkative, with a shrill and sometimes scolding sound which could be heard well out on the Lakes by which they nested. Mass migrations of the birds darkened the sky, obscuring the sun. The birds were caught in nets, knocked down by poles or shot. It would seem that it was in the 1860s that the indiscriminate killing of the passenger pigeon began, and peaked in 1878 when the great colony near Petoskey, Michigan was exterminated. One account says that five freight car loads of pigeons left from the town every day for thirty days. After that, the number of passenger pigeon declined dramatically. The last band was found in St. Vincent, Quebec in 1907. They were all killed. The Michigan passenger pigeon is now extinct. By 1890, in addition to the extermination of the passenger pigeon, fishing had pretty well died out in the Great Lakes, especially compared to levels previously experienced. The introduction of the gill net to the Great Lakes in 1866 was a primary cause of this over exploitation.
Source: *Shingle Shavers and Berry Pickers,* Oliver Raymond.

[90] The Northern Journal, Spring 2006, Volume IV, Issue II.

The mills were shut down during this week.[91] Generally, band concerts and parades were events that accompanied Memorial Day and May Day celebrations. In 1879 there was the formal opening of the Maltz Opera House in Alpena.[92]

Other entertainment included tent shows that would occasionally come to town from the disembarking steamers and present plays such as *Uncle Tom's Cabin*. The Knights of Macabees was a very active group in towns surrounding the Great Lakes and often gave tent shows sponsored by the Ladies of the Macabees. Circuses also made visits to northern Michigan towns. Popular ones of the era were the McConkey S. Circus and Matt Wixom's Circus. It is not known if any of these circuses actually visited Alcona, but they were known to stop at towns farther south in Michigan. During this period, town meetings in villages such as Alcona were always held at night after or close to a full moon so that there was adequate light for the trip to and from the meeting.

In the 1880s, a new hobby was soon to grip the residents of Alcona, the bicycle. So popular was bicycling among the town's people that a Bicycle Club was formed. A five mile plank and cinder path was constructed between Alcona and the town of Black River

---

[91] Sterline, Elrita M. *First Fifty Years of Harrisville.* Central Michigan University, 1967; Clarke Historical Library, Mount Pleasant, Michigan.
[92] The Northern Journal, Spring 2006, Volume IV, Issue II.

to accommodate this new sport. A corduroy road was also built seven miles south to Harrisville made of three to six inch diameter cedar logs eight to ten feet wide. Evidence of these roads is still visible today with deteriorating cedar logs still in place. Corduroy roads were made by cutting down trees of small diameter and laying the spindly logs close together and parallel to each other. At times, some dirt might be thrown over them to stabilize and keep them in place. However, if the road was traveling through long marsh, it would often be just bare logs. Getting stuck in the low spots or mud was a common occurrence if traveling by wagon. When that happened the unfortunate traveler might have to wait for help if none was readily available. To free the wagon, the men would put both teams on one wagon and with poles that were cut from the nearby forest, they would pry the wheels up so that the horses could move the wagon.[93]

As Alcona blossomed so did the method of transporting mail. Originally, the northeastern shore of Lake Huron was served by mail runners on foot between ports. They were stout Frenchmen and "half-breed" Indians who were considered strong and had the endurance to "blaze trails" and run along the shoreline, swim rivers and track the established Indian trails to deliver mail up and

[93] *Birchbark Belles, Women on the Michigan Frontier*, edited by Larry B. Massie, The Priscilla Press, Allegan Forest, Michigan, 1993

down the coast between ship "stops." Indian dogsleds that were used to haul the mail in the winter were called a "traineau" and were generally pulled by four dogs.[94]   The dogs were fed hot cornmeal because meat was too heavy to carry.[95] Seth Willie, an Indian "half-breed" had the government shoreline mail contract in 1859 along the northeastern shore of Michigan.[96]

There was a stage line run by Daniel Carter between Alpena and Bay City in 1865, but it was unreliable due to the poor roadways and inadequate bridges.   Carter built a bridge across Thunder River in 1865 on contract with G.N. Fletcher, which was quite a feat. More reliable transportation by boat started around the year 1860.[97] In addition to these advances in transportation, the first telegraph was constructed in Alpena in 1879, and in 1881, a small electric plant was in operation.[98]   But, it was the coming of the steamship, particularly the Steamship *Marine City* in 1875 that revolutionized travel and availability of commodities to Alcona.

Here is another account from a Michigan pioneer:

---

[94] Sterling, Elrita M. *First Fifty Years of Harrisville,* Central Michigan University, 1967; Clarke Historical Library, Mount Pleasant, Michigan.
[95] Schelley, Marie, *Alcona, a Ghost Town*. Central Michigan University, 1967; Clarke Historical Library, Mount Pleasant, Michigan.
[96] Sterling, Erlita M. *First Fifty Years of Harrisville*
[97] Alpena County Opens to Settlement, David D. Oliver and A History of Alpena Co, The Northern Journal, Volume IV, Issue I, Winter 2006, page 27)
[98] The Northern Journal, Spring 2006, Volume IV, Issue II

The first year we were here we had to go forty miles for our mail and a letter from the east coast cost us twenty-five cents. We had to pay twenty dollars per barrel for flour and forty dollars per barrel for what was to be "one hog port." The hog that was in one barrel that we bought had three heads and feet to match. Indian squaws often speared sturgeon nearby that would weigh all the way up to sixty to one hundred pounds.[99]

MAPLE SYRUP HARVESTING

Maple syrup harvesting was a significant event in Michigan. The syrup that was made for table use was boiled until it was very thick. This prevented its getting sour. The syrup intended for summer use would be put into jugs and buried in the ground two or three feet deep. This would keep it about a year.[100] It was often a trade item.

Here is an account from one maple syrup camp:

One time, a party of five ladies and five gentlemen were invited to the maple sugar camp. Each lady brought a frying pan in which to cook and turn

---

[99] *Birchbark Belles, Women on the Michigan Frontier*, edited by Larry B. Massie, The Priscilla Press, Allegan Forest, Michigan, 1993
[100] *Birchbark Belles, Women on the Michigan Frontier*, edited by Larry B. Massie, The Priscilla Press, Allegan Forest, Michigan, 1993.

'les crepes' or pancakes, which were to be the special feature in fun of the occasion. We were notified that no girl was fitted to be married until she could turn crepes. Naturally, all were desirous to try their skill in that direction whether matrimonially inclined or not. The gentlemen of the party tried their hand at it as well as the ladies. To turn a crepe, it was dexterously tossed in the air and expected to land the other side up back in the pan. Great fun was occasioned by this event. These crepes turned and flew everywhere but where we wanted them. Many fell into the fire. You may imagine the sport all this afforded. In due time, a nice dinner was prepared. We had partridges roasted on sticks before the fire, rabbits and stuffed squirrel, cooked French fashion; and finally had as many crepes with syrup as we desired. Everyone departed with a bark of wax and sugar cakes.[101]

The last run of maple syrup sap was converted into sugar for the making of beer. Some of it was boiled thick enough to turn into vinegar. To make beer, princess pine, wintergreen and squaw berries, hemlock bows, sarsaparilla and various other items were collected from the forest and boiled in lots of water. The mixture was then strained, sweetened and put in a wooden tub. Hop yeast was mixed in, and a few hours later it would begin to ferment. It was ready to drink

---

[101] Ibid

in a day or two.   The beer was considered a good spring medicine and a delicious drink.[102]

THE GENERAL STORE

The general store was more than just a place to buy food. It was a gathering place during the 19th century where warm and friendly people met to discuss news and politics and catch up on all that was happening locally and nationally. To a young child growing up on the frontier, just a trip to town was a special treat, but a trip to the store was a time of wonder.   The store was a delight for the senses and a place where the 'luxuries' only dreamed about could become reality.

Della Lutes, a farm girl who grew up in Michigan during the final decades of the 19th century writes about her experiences in the book *Country Kitchen.*

> I could not have been more than six at my earliest remembrance of going to town with him (her dad).....To me it seems the epitome of plenty and luxury. The eye was thrilled and the

---

[102] Ibid

nose teased by a diversity of both strange and the familiar[103].

So, what might the store have been like? It carried just about everything that the people in the area could need. Quite often it also served as the town's post office and general gathering place where a warm stove, checkerboards and barrels full of all kinds of things beckoned the townspeople or farmers.[104]

Bulk food, clothing and hardware were all found at the store. Quite often the entire first floor was used to display the merchandise and much was done to maximize the storage and display of the items. Goods such as coffee, flour, sugar, crackers, pickles, spices, kerosene and other supplies were purchased by the owner of the store in bulk quantities with the amount desired by the customer measured out into bags or jugs. There were some pre-packaged food such as sardines, oysters and canned peaches. Larger items such as equipment for the farm or for the home (such as sewing machines and stoves) had to be "special" ordered. Typically, the store would issue in-store credit for a family who would bring butter and eggs to sell.[105]

---

[103] *The Country Kitchen*, Della T. Lutes, Wayne State University Press, pp. 72.

[104] Greteman Brothers' General Store, Living History Farms, www. Lhf.org

[105] Ibid

Della Lutes, goes on to describe the store in *The Country Kitchen.*

> Beyond the counter ran down one side of the room, and a glass showcase displayed more delicate goods on the other side, such, for instance, as jars of stick candy – cinnamon, peppermint, wintergreen and horehound....Behind these were shelves of which stored overalls wampuses[106], shoes, bolts of calico and muslin and, a little further down, dishes....
>
> It was my father's custom, after meeting the storekeeper, to step up to the cheese box, take the knife, and cut for themselves a generous wedge of cheese with a smaller one for children and dip into the barrel for a handful of crackers and stride back and forth around to where the upturned boxes and nail kegs made seating accommodations and sit beside the potbellied, rusty stove at the back of the store. There, often, the storekeeper would join us to discuss the price of groceries, potatoes, butter, eggs and the terms of trade as well as exchange news and politics and the national conditions generally.[107]

---

[106] A wampus, also known as a wamus, is a durable, coarse outer jacket. http://dictionary.reference.com/search?q=wamus
[107] *The Country Kitchen*, Della T. Lutes, Wayne State University Press, pp.71-73.

A SIMPLE CHRISTMAS

Christmas became a special affair in nineteenth century Michigan. At that time, the holiday had not been celebrated that long. The Puritans of Massachusetts actually banned any observance of Christmas and anyone caught celebrating or observing the holiday was fined. By the early 1800s though, there was some decoration of Christmas trees throughout the country, a tradition that German immigrants helped spread across the American continent in the early 1800s. Prior to the Civil War, the celebration of Christmas also divided the North and South. There were many in the North who saw it as a sin to celebrate Christmas. In the South though, Christmas was an important part of the social season.[108]

After the Civil War, however, the traditions associated with Christmas spread across the country, and by the end of the nineteenth century, Americans were decorating trees, caroling, baking and shopping. Alcona was no exception.

Once again, we turn to the young Michigan pioneer girl, Della Lutes, to get an idea of what Christmas was like in the wilds of Michigan.

---

[108] Hoover Library, *An American Christmas*, http://hoover.archives.gov/exhibits/AmChristmas

An orange in the toe of the stocking, a well-polished apple oddly resembling those in our own cellar, a stick or two of peppermint, cinnamon, or horehound candy, constituted the contents of the average stocking, and quite satisfying they were, too....

Christmas day was lifted, in our home, only a few degrees above the plane of any other simple holiday.

On the day before Christmas my father came home with a large, fat goose, dressed and drawn, dangling its long neck around his feet.

The table was spread with the second best cloth of white linen, the best being reserved for the later and greater occasion of my father's birthday....We did not even use the gold-banded china for Christmas, but the sprigged rose pattern that my mother had bought not so long ago with carefully hoarded egg money.

Dessert, of course, on Christmas Day consisted of plum pudding and plum pudding only.[109]

NATIVE AMERICANS

In the 1600s the Native American population of Michigan was estimated at about 15,000, with 12,000 living in the southern portion of the Lower Peninsula. The

---

[109] *The Country Kitchen*, Della T. Lutes, Wayne State University Press, pp.241, 244 and 248.

three major groups were the Pottawatomie, the Ottawa, and the Ojibwa also known as Chippewa. They were all closely related Algonquian-speaking people. Collectively, they defeated the war prone Sauks.[110] The Sauks around Alcona were wiped out in the early 1600s by a series of coordinated attacks planned by the Ottawa, Pottawatomies, Menominee, Chippewa, and the Six Nation Tribes from Canada. The Six Nations came from the north and other Indian tribes came from the west and south and coordinated attacks literally massacring all but a small number of Sauk families.[111] There were other smaller groups living in the state, and they included the Miami, the Menominee, and the Iroquoian-speaking Wyandotte. The latter settled near what is now the City of Detroit.[112] The Cass Treaty of Saginaw of 1819 ceded all the land from Thunder Bay River, near present day Alpena, and to the southwest of Kalamazoo from the Indians.[113]

The groups in southern Michigan relied mostly on agriculture while the Chippewa in the northern areas, where the weather was cooler, depended more on fishing and hunting. It was the Ottawa that lived

---

[110] Http://encarta.msn.com/text_761572168_45/michigan.html

[111] Sterling, Elrita M. *First Fifty Years of Harrisville*, Central Michigan University, 1967; Clarke Historical Library, Mount Pleasant, Michigan and Schelley, Marie. *Alcona, a Ghost Town*. Central Michigan University, 1967; Clarke Historical Library, Mount Pleasant, Michigan.

[112] Http://encarta.msn.com/text_761572168_45/michigan.html

[113] Sterling, Elrita M., *First Fifty Years of Harrisville*. Central Michigan University, 1967; Clarke Historical Library, Mount Pleasant, Michigan.

between these two groups who were mostly traders.[114]   In the area of Alcona, the Chippewa tapped maple trees and made sugar for trade.   They also trapped minks, martins, otters, fishers, cougars, lynx, bobcat, wolves, fox and hunted deer, elk and moose.[115]   There were several hundred Native Americans living in Northeast Michigan with about 200-300 living in the general Alcona area in the 1840 - 1880s.   [116]   Giant skeletons of earlier inhabitants, estimated to be seven feet tall, found at the mouth of Devil's River near Ossineke and near Greenbush, establish much earlier habitations of different groups as well.

The tribes living in the northern part of the state depended on fishing and hunting to survive.   The Chippewa often lived at the mouths of rivers and existed on nothing but fish, even though there was tillable land suitable for raising corn and excellent hunting

---

[114] Http://encarta.msn.com/text_761572168_45/michigan.html

[115] In 1843 a hunter and trapper by the name of Youngs was hired to stay in the woods of Alpena County all winter to study the nature and habits of the animals.   Otter, beaver, lynx, martin, raccoon, fish, bear and mink were plentiful in the area.
Alpena County Opens to Settlement, David D. Oliver and *A History of Alpena Co.*, The Northern Journal, Volume IV, Issue I, Winter 2006, page 26.

[116] The Indians of the area, who somehow survived the white man's diseases, often lived a long time, some even living to be 100 years old.   One of the early pioneers in Michigan, William R. McCormick, of Bay City, tells of meeting an Indian in what he thought was 1835 and asking him his age. "He said he thought he was a great deal over one hundred years old. His faculties were as bright as those of a man of fifty." *Who Were the Michigan Saukes and What is Their Place in History?* Compiled by Nelson Yoder, The Northern Journal, Volume IV, Issue I, Winter 2006, page 14.

grounds nearby.[117]   They were known to use attractive amulets for exchange.[118]

The villages that the Indians lived in were most often located along travel routes and waterways.   Many of the white settlers thought that the ways of the Natives were strange and, very often, barbaric.   There were some, however, who were more understanding.   For example, missionaries often would intervene in treaty negotiations in an attempt to make sure that the Native people were treated fairly. By the year 1838, almost all of the Native villages in Michigan's Lower Peninsula had been abandoned.[119]

NATIVE FOOD SOURCES

Lake sturgeon used to be plentiful in Michigan, and especially in the waters off Alcona. They could easily be caught as they moved up rivers and streams. Great Lakes sturgeon would grow on average about six to eight feet long and were so numerous around Sturgeon Point that they were considered pests. When they would spawn at "strawberry time," people, including the life saving crew, would spear them by the hundreds and bring them on shore to die as they were considered a pest because they would damage the fishing

---

[117] The Northern Journal, Spring, 2006, Volume IV, Issue II
[118] The Besser Museum of Alpena has a collection found in Negwegon, north of the Town of Alcona and Black River.
[119] Native American History in Michigan.

nets.[120] The average sturgeon weighed about 60 pounds and a few of them would feed an entire tribe. The Indians had various means with which they captured fish. They fashioned fish hooks from bone, wood, or copper before white men came with their fabricated metal hooks. The native residents used hemp and fiber of the basswood bark to make lines, and they even used lures. The lures were hard and dyed and placed inside a small fish. Using the lure they were able to take many lake trout. As far back as 1709, an explorer reports that the natives were using small porcelain-like fish, most likely made of shell, which they placed in the water attached to the end of a line. [121]

Nets were also used to catch fish. They were made of wild hemp, nettles, basswood bark and other tough fibers. Cedar wood was used to buoy the nets, and stones were placed at the bottom to weight the net down. Very large catches were brought in this way. The Chippewa could catch as many as a hundred whitefish in one net. Weirs were constructed on many of the streams and rivers by the Chippewa. A weir is a simple barricade with an opening to allow fish to swim upstream. When the fish attempted to return to the

---

[120] Swenson, Helen. *Sturgeon Point Coast Guard Station.* Central Michigan University, 1967; Clarke Historical Library, Mount Pleasant, Michigan.
[121] The Northern Journal, Spring, 2006, Volume IV, Issue II. Great Lakes sturgeon are now an endangered species.

lake, the opening was barricaded, making the fish easy prey for spears or nets. [122]

In 1832, an army officer described a device that was used by the Chippewa for taking sturgeon along the Great Lakes. The Chippewa would fish with long poles which had sturdy hooks secured to the ends. The pole would be poked around in the river or lake water until a fish was felt and then the Indian would give a violent upward heave hoisting the fish out of the water. The fish were never taken indiscriminately. Generally, the Indians killed only for food. [123]

The following is a pioneer account of the Northern Michigan Indian:

> The Indian does not know what regular meal hours are; he gorges himself with food when he can and then fasts until he again finds something to satisfy his appetite; wolves do the same thing. But the Indian is the most philosophic of men. He has few needs, and correspondingly few desires. Civilization has no hold on him. He is ignorant of and despises its comforts. It is not however that the native of the new world lacks natural aptitude; his nature seems obstinately to reject our ideas and our arts. Lying on his blanket in the smoke of his hut the Indian

---

[122] Ibid. Some spears were really little more than a long (18-20 ft) pole on which was fastened a flat, sharp bone. When the fish was hit, the dart, which was pierced and attached to a cord, separated from the pole and remained in the fish.

[123] Ibid.

regards with scorn the comfortable dwelling of the European. As for him, he takes a proud pleasure in his misery and his heart swells and lifts at the evidences of his barbarian independence. He smiles bitterly on seeing us torment our lives to acquire useless riches. What we call industry he calls shameful servitude. He compares the laborer to the ox painfully plowing his furrow. What we call the comforts of life he calls children's toys and women's playthings. He envies us only our weapons. When a man can shelter his head at night under a tent of foliage, when he can light a fire to drive off the mosquitoes in summer and protect himself from cold in the winter, when his dogs are good and the country full of game, what more could he ask of the Eternal Being[124].

Another account can be summarized as follows:

My father brought home an Indian named Jack and he seemed nearly dead. When my mother had tried all remedies without his reviving, she thought he was dying and taking her rosary and kneeling by his side began to repeat the prayer for the dying. Soon Jack opened his eyes and reached a feeble hand, took the crucifix and kissed it. Mother then prayed for the

---

[124] *The Making of Michigan 1820-1860 A Pioneer Anthology*, edited by Justin L. Kestenbaum, Wayne State University Press, 1990.

restoration of the living and Jack joined in a feeble voice. He proved to be a Canadian half-breed and had been baptized a Catholic. A bond of friendship sprang up between Jack and the family and it proved a great blessing to us poor white people who were near the point of starving. Jack brought down with his gun plenty of game and distributed amongst the families that were needy. He also took medicines that he had made of roots and herbs to those that were ill and there were many. These roots and herbs cured most of us. He taught our men and boys to make traps to catch game for ammunition was too expensive to be had at all times. Jack made whistles for us as children that he made out of basswood. One night my mother and brother heard a woman screaming down near the creek. They hastened in that direction as best they could in the pitchy darkness and when they arrived a hand was laid upon them and in silence they waited. Soon the screams were heard again and Jack's gun fell a large panther some feet away. Jack had understood the screams and saved their lives. He taught the boys how to make splint brooms out of hickory saplings. He showed them how the waste splints were treasured for kindling as he started fires with flint and steel and punk by striking the flint on steel and having a piece of plank under to catch the sparks. Soon the splinters would be added and then the wood. Previously mother would often send us several miles to get coals from our neighbors to start fires if our fires went out. Jack showed us a way to start a fire right on our farm. Out by a stump, he put stones in a hollow on the ground where we kept coals covered with ashes which maintained our fires without them going out.[125]

Many residents of the area had firearms mostly with unrifled barrels fired by flintlock mechanisms and later "cap and ball" Civil War rifled Springfield and Sharps carbines. Even by 1880, only the well-heeled had the early center fire Henry 44s or Winchester Repeaters. Pistols were another matter with many armed with both Civil War Ball and Cap .36 caliber six shooters, derringers and by 1880, with brass cartridge six shooters. There were virtually no gun regulations, yet homicides were rare or at least unreported in Northern Michigan. Although strychnine poisoning was confirmed in three murders and suspected in other possible murders over the course of 15 years in Alpena towards the end of the 19th century.[126]

In 1871, only Native American runners brought winter mail when the Great Lakes were too dangerous with ice to ply by ship. By 1883, there were mail boats that brought correspondence to Alcona three times a week,

[125] *Birchbark Belles, Women on the Michigan Frontier*, edited by Larry B. Massie, The Priscilla Press, Allegan Forest, Michigan, 1993, p. 204
[126] *The Murder of Baby Teeple*, Ann Rahamut, The Northern Journal, Spirng 2007, Volume V, Issue II, p. 29-35

except in the winter. These were in addition to the daily steamers. It was usually April before the water was free enough of ice to navigate Lake Huron. Lighthouses were not lit until April and continued to be lit until mid-December. During the winter months, skaters would often glide between the towns on Lake Huron, from Alcona to Harrisville or north to Black River.

Education was very basic for the students when the two schools in the Alcona area consolidated in 1887 into an elongated one room "District" school house on top of Mt. Joy, a half mile west of Alcona. A sixth grade education was considered a major achievement. During 1893, 125 pupils attended the school (most of which surely griped about the hike up the formidable hill behind Alcona). Mt. Joy School still stands today and is used as a private residence.

Mt. Joy was known primarily for housing a graveyard upon its peak. Many Alcona citizens rest in peace there. A man by the name of Newton Edwards may have been the reason why Mt. Joy got its name. Mr. Edwards, a harness maker by trade and an Ontario Canadian native, came across Lake Huron to work for the Alger Smith Company (See tintype photograph of Newton Edward in his shop in Alcona later in this publication, Figure 8, Page 85). By 1893, when the Alcona area had almost exhausted its forest reserves, he was named "the Mayor of Ghost Town" by

Charles Mills of the Village of Lincoln, a thriving farming town twelve miles inland. Newt received a gold medal for this honor, which he wore with pride. He was also known for giving thrilling sleigh rides to children down the steep graveyard hill behind Alcona during the winters with the children gleefully yelling. Hence the hill became known as Mt. Joy. He is buried on that hill with his bywords, "That's right, that's right."[127]

---

[127] Alcona County Review records

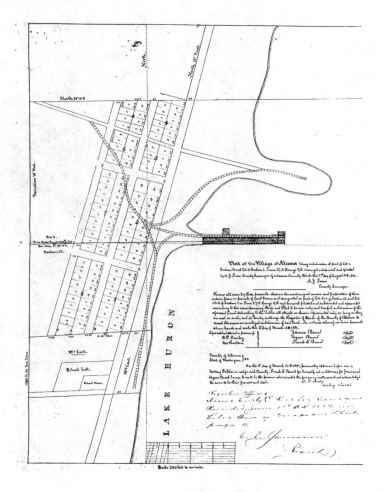

Figure One

Figure of old Alcona with its narrow gauge railroad and substantial pier at Alcona Pointe

Compliments of Thomas Maxwell of Alcona Pointe.

ALBYN

Figure Two

A painting of a home of the Superintendent of Alger
Smith Company

Compliments of Gordon Bennett III of Black River, President of the
Alcona Historic Society.

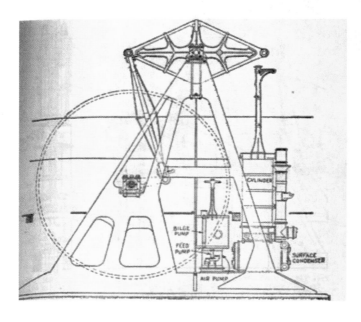

Figure Three

The vertical or "walking-beam" engine

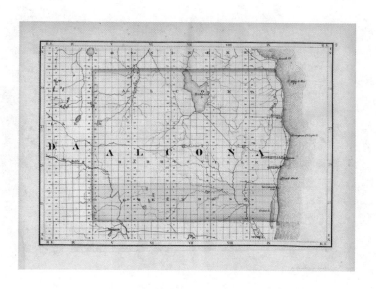

Figure Four

Original map, 1880, of area of Alcona

Figure Five

Painting of The Town of Alcona in 1880 with the famous
tugboat *Vulcan* by Robert McGreevy
Note the locomotive on the dock in the background and
the log aft in the foreground.

Compliments of the Robert Lowell Bunting Foundation

Figure Six

Painting of the *Neshoto* shortly before she sank off Sturgeon Point, Michigan, three miles south of Alcona by Robert McGreevy

Note the Sturgeon Point Lighthouse in the background.

Compliments of Robert Lowell Bunting Foundation

81

Sidewheel str. Mar...

Sturgeon Point, 1880

Figure Seven

The _Marine City_ by Robert McGreevy

Note the US Lifesaving Station next to the lighthouse, and the town of Alcona on the right.

Compliments of The Robert Lowell Bunting Foundation

All that is left of the Town of Alcona from a photograph
taken in the 1920s showing one of the main streets.

Figure Eight

Newt Edwards, Mayor of ghost town of Alcona

85

Figure Nine

Lifesaving crew launching a surfboat similar to the one used in the Marine City disaster

Painting by Robert McGreevy

Figure Ten

Remains of the Marine City, 2007

The Village of Alcona would fade into
obscurity by the end of the 19th century.
Lumbering became unsustainable with over-
harvesting. In 1893, a fire engulfed the
shingle and timber mills of Alcona leaving vast
unemployment in its wake, hastening its
decline.[128] With the razing of the mills in
conjunction with the lack of timber, the
population dwindled. Tourism was a long way
off as were the owners of summer lake front
homes with enough leisure time to enjoy the
sugar sands of Alcona's pristine bay. The lake
front land was considered unproductive and
worthless. Some houses were moved inland
to farms, others torn down, sold, recycled or
simply abandoned. (There are functional
farm houses today well inland that were once
in the town of Alcona, as well as homes in
Harrisville brought across the icy shores of
Lake Huron during the winter that are
occupied to this day.) The lumber companies
and jobs ventured further north seeking more
virgin timber to satisfy young America's
insatiable appetite for wood to build homes
and cities. Today, nothing remains of the
Village of Alcona but an occasional lilac bush
and substantial wooden pier stumps still
visible beneath the quiet waters of the cove

---

[128] Significantly, twenty years earlier, fire caused economic disaster in
Harrisville when the primary mill burned to the ground in 1873. Suspiciously,
this coincided the market crash of lumber in 1873. A Mr. Hensler, a lumber
dealer in the northeast Michigan area, committed suicide over his losses.
Sterling, Elrita M. *First Fifty Years of Harrisville*. Central Michigan
University, 1967; Clarke Historical Library, Mount Pleasant, Michigan.

in Lake Huron. Back country stumps, some of which are four to five feet in diameter, are still discernable where once stood the tall, majestic white pine forests. Second and third growth forests now have obliterated evidence of the once vibrant town.

LIFE IN THE 1880S

In the 1880s, an unskilled laborer's wages were $1.50 to $1.60 a day (often a twelve hour day). That compares to $7.00 per hour set by law for unskilled labor in Michigan in 2006. Prices for goods then were also much lower. In the 1880s, backgammon boards were $1.80, checkers were 15 cents, dolls cost from 50 cents to 80 cents, jacks were 30 cents, kaleidoscopes 50 cents, a small bag of marbles 65 cents, paint boxes between 21 cents and 50 cents, scrapbooks 85 cents, whistles 45 cents, a pack of cards 20 cents, a complete croquet set $2.10, one pound of chocolate 35 cents, and licorice 5 cents.[129]

Growing up in Michigan in the 1880s was in some ways very different than it is now, but in some ways similar. In the 1880s, chores for girls included sewing, cleaning, washing clothes, churning butter, cooking, canning and weeding the garden. Chores for boys included planting, harvesting and

---

[129] Kids History from Michigan Time Traveler, Lansing Newspapers and Education, Inc., provided by the Lansing State Journal and the Michigan Historical Center Foundation.

chopping wood. Both girls and boys helped with milking cows, picking fruit, gathering eggs, and tending the garden. During the 1880s, not all children attended school on a regular basis for a variety of reasons: farm work, work in mills, mines and factories, and distance from the school. (Children walked or rode horses to school at this time.) It wasn't until 1883 that children were required by law to attend school on a regular basis.[130] In the year 1905, only six percent of all Americans had graduated from high school.[131]

In the 1880s children enjoyed many of the same activities that they currently enjoy. They liked outdoor activities, horseback riding, skating, bicycling, reading, marbles, picnics, holiday celebrations and fairs. One holiday that was celebrated in a fashion fairly similar to today was the 4th of July. The celebration in the 1880s would include fireworks, speeches, parades, reading the Declaration of Independence, bands, races, sports, picnics and games. Of course, there were also a few activities then that are not common today, such as climbing greased poles, chasing greased pigs, sack races and potato races, which entailed pushing a potato on the ground with your nose to a finish line. Ice cream in the summer was also a big deal because modern refrigeration methods were

---

[130] Lansing Newspapers in Education, Inc. Provided by the *Lansing State Journal* and the Michigan Historical Center.
[131] The Northern Journal, Spring, 2006, Volume IV, Issue II.

not available. Instead, ice would be cut out of the lakes and rivers during the winter and taken to an icehouse where it was stored in sawdust for use during the warmer months.[132]

As is always the case, books from this period reflected the society of the day and helped give people a better understanding of the world in which they lived. Books written during this time period included *Portrait of a Lady* by Henry James which was published in 1881 and centered on the psychological story of an American woman inheriting money and living in Europe, Mark Twain's *Huckleberry Finn* which was published in 1885 and *Ramona* and *A Century of Dishonor* by Helen Hunt Jackson. *Ramona* was a bestseller in 1884. The latter two books described the harsh treatment of Native Americans by the U.S. Government. All were progressive books for the time. [133]

Immigration to the United States changed somewhat in the 1880s. During that decade, 5,248,568 immigrants came to the United States. Most came from northern and western Europe, but an increasing number came from southern and eastern Europe. During this time, steamship travel made the journey to America faster and safer (and more comfortable) for the immigrants. The Foran

---

[132] Lansing Newspapers in Education, Inc. Provided by the *Lansing State Journal* and the Michigan Historical Center.
[133] Kingwood College, American Cultural History, The 19th Century Decades Pages, http://kclibrary.nhmccd.edu/19thcentury1880.htm

Act of 1885 made it illegal for American industry to contract foreign labor. The Chinese Exclusion Act of 1882 attempted to stop the Chinese from entering the country. The padrone, or labor boss, encouraged Italians and Greeks to come to the United States for jobs. The padrone system did well during this time period and helped cause a shift in immigration. The "old immigrants" such as the British, Irish, Scotch, Scandinavian and German were being outnumbered by those of different nationalities.[134]

During the 1880s, children attended frontier schools that would be considered primitive by today's standards, with far less comfort for both the teacher and the students. Many times a one-room schoolhouse lacked even a blackboard. Students were sometimes expected to provide their own books so that they ended up learning lessons from a variety of sources using whatever was available, even if badly dog-eared. Despite the challenges, teachers were not paid much. The average salary for women was $54.50 a year and for men it was $71.40. If available, the McGuffey texts were used during this time period. They proposed to teach morality, reading and patriotism along with history.[135]

Discipline in the schools was very strict. Children who misbehaved might have to be

[134] Ibid
[135] Ibid

switched, sit in a locked, dark closet or sit in front of the class wearing a dunce cap. Students who were left handed were forced to write with their right hands. Just getting to school could be hazardous. In January 1888, in what became known as the "schoolchildren blizzard," many children died while attempting to get home from school on the Nebraska Plains.[136]

Other interesting news items of note during the 1880s include the following:

- The most popular names for boys were John and William and for girls, Mary and Anna.
- There were over 600 lynchings of African Americans mostly in the South, yet only 200 homicides were considered reportable nationwide.
- A ten story building was built in Chicago.
- Clara Barton organized the Red Cross.
- In Boston, 1882, electric incandescent light bulbs provided the lighting for a production of Gilbert and Sullivan's *Iolanthe*. This was the first such use of the new technology.[137] Prior to this, kerosene coal oil or whale oil was used in lamps. It was widely used in towns such as Alcona and was the sole source

---

[136] Ibid
[137] Ibid

for lighting on steamers like the *Marine City*.[138]

The 1880s also saw operas and operettas, particularly those by Gilbert and Sullivan, touring the country. Other entertainment included "The Buffalo Bill Wild West show" which opened on July 4, 1883. Lillian Russell began her rise to operatic stardom during this time. Shapely women showed as much leg as the law and convention would allow (which was not a lot) and witty humor was the mainstay. During this decade, a dance developed similar to the can-can and vaudeville was born. Vaudeville shows were popular. Andrew Carnegie also opened his first public library during this time. Thomas Edison incorporated ideas and music from others into an improved phonograph that used wax cylinders in 1888. Other innovations during the period included modern conveniences such as running water, gas, electricity, the flushable toilet, and sewer systems to some homes in larger cities. Except for the wealthy, though, modern plumbing was still not accessible. Outhouses and tin bathing tubs which were filled with water heated on a stove and used by multiple

---

[138] Kerosene is commonly obtained in the fractional distillation of petroleum, but it has also been recovered from other sources, such as coal, oil shale, and wood. It was first refined from coal in 1846 by Atlantic Canada's Abraham Gesner. This was the founding of the modern petroleum industry. At one time kerosene was the most important refinery product because of its use in lamps. Now it is most noted for its use as a carrier in insecticide sprays and as a fuel in jet engines. http://www.answers.com/topic/kerosene.

persons were still common.[139]   The pages of an out of date Sears catalog would often be used in an outhouse for toilet paper.

The American diet, consisting mainly of potatoes, cabbage and, at times, salt pork and beans, diversified during the 1880s. Refrigerated railway cars using large blocks of ice made it possible to ship grapefruit from Florida, citrus from California and meat from Chicago's slaughterhouses to any place with access to a rail line. Previously considered poisonous, tomatoes now made it into the kitchen and in 1886, Coca Cola made its entrance as a "brain and nerve" tonic.   It actually contained cocaine at that time.[140]

Not only did a greater variety of food become more accessible during this time period, so did fashion. Mail order houses such as Montgomery Ward and Sears, Roebuck opened and provided the same clothes already available to women in the east to those in the Midwest.   As men's clothing became more casual and fashionable, women wore more and more elaborate dresses. The bustle, a wire cage, was fastened around the waist of a dress and extended out in back of the dress. Corsets, tightly laced, were also popular and gave women tiny waists, but little room to breathe.[141]

---

[139] Kingwood College, American Cultural History, The 19th Century Decades Pages, http://kclibrary.nhmccd.edu/19thcentury1880.htm
[140] Ibid
[141] Ibid

Such elaborate dress surely limited the exercise options for women. However, girls did participate in tennis, croquet, bowling and seaside bathing. Around 50,000 Americans owned bicycles by the year 1884, and sports such as baseball, golf, roller skating and football were also enjoyed. Indoors, the stereoscope was a popular form of entertainment. [142] The stereoscope was a side by side post card size print of a subject or scene and provided viewers a perception of depth when viewed through a lens.

Constance Fenimore Woolson, the grand niece of James Fenimore Cooper, published her first collection of short-stories in 1875. The collection was titled *Castle Nowhere: Lake-Country Sketches* and included her best pieces set in the Great Lakes region. She made her debut as a novelist in 1880 with *Anne*. *Anne* was first serialized in *Harper's New Monthly Magazine* in the 1880s and then published in volume form two years later.[143]

In science and technology, the Brooklyn Bridge opened as the longest suspension bridge in the world. The internal combustion engine was developed, and the first electric automobile was designed in 1887. Thomas Edison developed the first electric power system in the world, the Edison Electric

---

[142] Ibid
[143] The Literary Encyclopedia,
www.litencyc.com/php/speople.php?rec=true&UID=4802

Illuminating Company, in 1882 using direct current. In medicine, the miasmatic theory of contagion was replaced by the infectious disease theory.[144] The miasmatic theory of contagion, held since the time of Hippocrates, was based on the belief that disease was "caused by miasmas, which were alterations of the atmosphere that arose from the earth and attacked the body."[145]

Socially, society in America was becoming more modern. Women took more roles outside the home and were given more opportunities in education, politics and work, but were not allowed to vote. Sadly, however, there were setbacks. The immigrants did not always blend successfully into American society. Anti-Catholicism and anti-Semitism started to take hold in communities across the country. During this decade in the South, African Americans were robbed of the rights as citizens that had been purportedly won after the Civil War through such tactics as violence, poll taxes, literacy tests, and intimidation. Tribal lands of the Native Americans were gradually eliminated by the Dawes Severalty Act of 1887. Yet, the same act provided for the introduction of

---

[144] Kingwood College, American Cultural History, The 19th Century Decades Pages, http://kclibrary.nhmccd.edu/19thcentury1880.htm

[145] The American Heritage Book of English Usage, 1996, Houghton Mifflin Company, www.bartleby.com/64/C004/020.html

Protestant and Catholic missionaries on reservations.[146]

LOVE AND ROMANCE IN THE 1880'S IN ALCONA

Weddings in Alcona during the Victorian period[147] were far simpler than they are now. The bride of the mid to late-1880s in rural America usually wore a dress made of cambric, wool or linen in a variety of colors. Few brides wore white because the dress would be used later for other events and for church. Many of the women would have had a warm, colorful shawl in paisley or plaid they owned and would have worn the day of their weddings. The shawl would then be used for christenings, social events and as an extra blanket during the winter. The warm shawl was more cherished than the wedding dress. Also, by 1890 the bustle disappeared from the American fashion scene.

The wedding day fashion for men included coats tailored with a special hole for the flower. After 1885, men generally wore gloves at formal events. [148]

The courtship practices that preceded the wedding during this time were far

---

[146] Kingwood College, American Cultural History, The 19th Century Decades Pages, http://kclibrary.nhmccd.edu/19thcentury1880.htm
[147] In England, the 1880's were part of the reign of Queen Victoria which became known as the Victorian Era.
[148] The Victorian Wedding, www.literary-liaisons.com/article003.html

different than they are today and had evolved over the years. Courtship and marriage revolved around rational needs and, supposedly, not lust, and a man ideally only married when he could support his new wife and a family with his income and possessions. Many believed that love developed as the marriage progressed – not before. During the 1800s, though, love started to become increasingly important. However, this love was not romantic love. That was seen as childish. What was sought, reportedly, was openness and sincerity.[149] Whether these sources are accurate is anyone's guess.

However, most couples did meet each other at social activities, such as church. These social activities gave couples much time and opportunity to get to know one another in a public, somewhat structured setting. Couples could still meet privately for walks or to talk in a parlor. Many couples supposedly refrained from having sexual relations prior to marriage due to the social pressures and customs of the day. In the 1770s, however, a century before, premarital pregnancies did occur and reached an all time high of thirty percent in the early U.S. After that, it is reported, such pregnancies were viewed as unacceptable and the premarital pregnancy

---

[149] The Historical Evolution of Dating in America, Natalie Flynn, www.oberline/edu/facutly/ndarling/transition/group21/history.html

rate decreased dramatically during the 1800's, according to this source. [150]

It was easier for a man to transition into marriage than a woman. The role of the man was still dominant. Women had a harder time with the transition because they often had to leave friends and family and move to a new house and, quite often, a new town.[151]

In the 1830s to 1880s courtship went through some changes. Gender roles became more important. Women, who were seen as morally upright, were given more authority over household duties and the raising of children. This separated women into a domestic role that also led to less social contact between younger boys and girls as the girls were taught household duties early on under the direct tutelage of their mothers or other older women in the family. Outside the home, men still remained the main authority and had more autonomy.[152]

The new structure seen in gender roles also led to more formality in courtships. Rings were exchanged to represent engagement and permission to marry was asked of the parents of the prospective. This new formality also saw the entrance of the white bridal gown and veil, representing purity. There was less emphasis on the physical aspects of courtship during this

---

[150] Ibid
[151] Ibid
[152] Ibid

100

period. Public physical expressions were looked down upon. Unmarried couples could still be passionate in private, but they were said to have refrained from direct sexual relations.[153]

In spite of all of the formality, romantic love played a much more important role than it had during colonial times. In fact, romantic love was seen as the main requirement for marriage. Because women relied almost exclusively on their husbands for financial security, romantic bonds were more important. Often women even tested their suitors to see if they would stay loyal. The tests included faking an illness, family disapproval and even breaking off the relationship to see if a suitor would persevere.[154]

From the 1880s to the 1920s courtship practices also changed. Women and men remained separated by their gender roles and rarely interacted. Separation was also seen as necessary so that a woman's chastity could be protected. Chaperones were common. Romantic love continued to grow in importance; however the man was seen as having the most intense emotions in the relationship. Formality was also still important. A couple had to be formally introduced, and the mother of the woman had to formally request a "call" from the man

---

[153] Ibid
[154] Ibid

101

before the couple was allowed to speak to one another. Most of the activities of courtship centered around the home of the woman and only took place if marriage was the goal of the man. [155]

Perhaps because of the formality and strict customs surrounding courtship in 1880, according to historian Robert L. Griswold, one marriage in 21 (fewer than five percent) ended in divorce. Divorce was also more difficult to obtain and was virtually impossible without a good reason such as adultery, abandonment, abuse or alcoholism.[156]

STEAMER HISTORY AND TRADE ON THE GREAT LAKES

In the town of Alcona, the passengers of the *Marine City* were embarking on their own ventures on August 29, 1880. These individuals were traveling to Harrisville, AuSable (Oscoda), Tawas, Detroit and ports to the south. Some were even from Ohio ports and were returning home after traveling up north on business or vacations.[157]

Earlier sailboat passengers traveling the Great lakes would each have tales to tell of the adventures experienced during the long

---

[155] Ibid

[156] www.divorcereform.org/rates.html

[157] In the 1880s tourists were known as "pleasurists."
Sterling, Elrita M. *First Fifty Years of Harrisville.* Central Michigan University, 1967; Clarke Historical Library, Mount Pleasant, Michigan.

trip from Detroit north on Lake Huron and then south to Chicago on Lake Michigan. They might have experienced long waits on the St. Clair flats, furious head winds off Thunder Bay, or long, seemingly endless calms at Mackinac or the Manitou Islands. A passenger might leave Detroit in June and not make it to Chicago until September.[158]

Detroit at this time was considered a desirable place to live. It was cheerful and picturesque. In town there were many half-breeds, French or English, children of white men married to Indian squaws. They played in the streets, rowed little skiffs in the river, played pranks along the shore and swam in the clean Detroit River. One account describes "the brimming river was bright in the morning sun and the road for a mile or two was thronged with Indians."[159]

In 1817, construction of the side-wheel steamers Ontario and Frontenac heralded the beginning of steam navigation on the Great Lakes. However, Lake vessel owners were slow to accept the steamboats. Trade in the 1820s was not great enough to justify the expense of building steamers. Thus, sailing craft continued to be built and operated by most vessel owners. In 1825, the Erie Canal was completed, giving a boost to the commerce and immigration of the Great Lakes

[158] *Birchbark Bells, Women on the Michigan Frontier*, edited by Larry B. Massie, The Priscilla Press, Allegan Forest, Michigan, 1993.
[159] Ibid

region[160]. The building of steamships now seemed justified by this increase in commerce and an increase in passenger traffic. 60 new steamboats were built in the four years after the Erie Canal was completed, a big increase when compared to the 25 steamboats that had been built in the 31 years before the Canal was opened. Most of the new steamships were built at Lake Erie ports.[161]

More than 100 steamers were in service on the Great Lakes by 1840. Most of the steamers were less than eight years old, and about 40 of them operated as ferries or on short local routes out of the larger ports. The rest of the steamers made trips from Buffalo to ports on the upper Lakes or from Niagara and Toronto to lower Lakes or St. Lawrence River destinations.[162] These would have

---

[160] Michigan was settled late in the history of the Great Lakes frontier. For the early pioneers moving westward, the land was difficult to access, heavily forested (Oak trees with circumferences of 9-15 feet were plentiful in the forests) and the land of uncertain reputation. *The Making of Michigan 1820-1860, A Pioneer Anthology*, edited by Justin L. Kestenbaum, Wayne State University Press, 1990.

[161] History and Development of Great Lakes Water Craft, http://www.mnhs.org/places/nationalregister/shipwrecks/mpdf/mpdf2.html

[162] The propeller Ontario ("propeller" distinguished from a sidewheeler propulsion, albeit also from steam power) was the first steam vessel to leave the Great Lakes for ocean navigation sailing from Buffalo for San Francisco. From 1850 to 1856 there were a number of vessels that made profitable trips from Canadian ports on Lake Ontario to ports in Europe. It was the steamer Dean Richmond that made the first direct clearance from Lake Michigan to Europe. The vessel left on July 19, 1857 and arrived at Liverpool on September 29th of that year. The C.J. Kershaw left Detroit on July 22, 1857 with a cargo of staves and reached Liverpool on September 5th. That same year the Maderia PET sailed from Detroit to Europe. In 1858 there were 15 vessels that left the Great Lakes for England with cargoes of lumber, staves, wheat and other grains. The next year, there were 16 vessels that entered the foreign trade from the Great Lakes to Europe. See "Beginning of Railroad Competition" originally published in 1910.

mostly been the larger steamers. The Erie Canal brought many new settlers, tens of thousands, to Buffalo each year looking for passage to the west. As a result, the population in cities that bordered the upper Lakes quadrupled in the eight years before 1840.[163]

Birchbark Belles, Women on the Michigan Frontier gives one account of a trip up the Detroit River in 1824 on a steamer:

> Presently, all were started by a large shrill whoop which thrilled the nerves like an electric shock. Peals of the most unearthly laughter from these Indians as they whooped and yelled into the air. They often bound gracefully along the shore whooping and calling out to us in their own language and trying the flight of their arrows in vain attempts to put some of their missiles on board. But the puffing steamer soon left them behind.
>
> As you approached north of Grosse Isle to Detroit you would come across very narrow farms only a few rods in width and extending about a mile or more with the farm house fronting along the river built in French style, large one story high with very steep roofs and dormer windows. (They were called French ribbon farms.) Many of them were painted white and all of them were half hidden by tall lilac and rosebushes. There would be a

---

[163] History and Development of Great Lakes Water Craft, http://www.mnhs.org/places/nationalregister/shipwrecks/mpdf/mpdf2.html

vegetable garden often extending to the waters edge with a wharf formed of a single plank which ran out into the river and was securely fastened. A stake was driven beside this little wharf for a canoe or sailboat.[164]

During the 1830s and 1840s, the demand for steamboats led to a rapid development in steamboat technology. The most common arrangement on the Great Lakes became the vertical or "walking beam" engine. This arrangement consisted of a "tall A-frame with a crosshead on top which rocked back and forth, attached to the cylinder on one end and the crankshaft on the other."[165](See figure 3, p. 76)

After the Civil War, coal started to be used as the fuel for the steamships. Prior to that, the steamers all burned cordwood. The boilers and engines of the steamers were very expensive. Because of that, they were often re-used or salvaged from other ships. They may have been used in three or more different hulls before they were worn out and of no more use.[166]

Through the 1880s-1890s, shipbuilders in Wayne County, Michigan built more ships than any other area in the country. However, the tonnage (carrying capacity) of the ships built at Bay County shipyards exceeded that

[164] *Birchbark Belles, Women on the Michigan Frontier*, edited by Larry B. Massie, The Priscilla Press, Allegan Forest, Michigan, 1993.
[165] http://www.mnhs.org/places/nationalregister/shipwrecks/mpdf/mpdf2.html
[166] Ibid

of the ships built in Wayne County. Shipyards in Bay City, Detroit and Grand Haven built 65 ships in 1890 alone. There were also many companies in Michigan that built marine engines, like P.F. Olds and Son in Lansing.[167]

Vessels like the *Marine City* were the most reliable and quickest way to travel in the northern regions of Michigan in 1880. Depending on class and accommodations, one-way passage to Detroit from Alcona ranged from $5 to $8. There were no lengthy, well-established or properly maintained roads or bridges. Local, very rough roads did exist by 1880 between Black River, Alcona, Harrisville, Lincoln and Hubbard Lake. (See 1880's map, Figure 4, p. 77) Early on in Alcona only the Pottawatomie and Kickapoo Indian Trails[168] were well-defined and could be regularly navigated on foot or horseback, but such trails could not reliably accommodate carriages or numerous pieces of luggage or supplies as the steamships readily could. In Negwegon, a pristine protected shoreline area north of Black River (5 miles north of Alcona), substantial finds of Indian amulets and other artifacts, including fish wiers made of rock in

[167]Great Lakes Maritime Time Line, Lansing Newspapers in Education, Inc. Provided by the *Lansing State Journal* and the Michigan Historical Center Foundation.
http://www.michigan.gov/documents/hal_mhc_mhm_schooner_tg_07-09-2002_92621_7.pdf
[168] The trails were marked by trees with a chip removed from them. This was called blazing the road. *Birchbark Belles, Women on the Michigan Frontier*, edited by Larry B. Massie, The Priscilla Press, Allegan Forest, Michigan, 1993.

Lake Huron, provide evidence of this early trade route and well established Indian presence closer to Alcona along these trails.

At the beginning of the second half of the 19th century, there were 95 steamboats, 45 propellers*, five barks, 93 brigs, 548 schooners and 100 sloops and scows on the entire chain of lakes[169]. In 1869, there were 121 side-wheel steamers, 140 propeller ships, 247 tugs, 175 sailing barks, 50 sailing brigs, and 223 sailing schooners and scows plying the Great Lakes.[170]

Steamers were basically the only reliable means of communicating with the outside world in the early development of the upper Great Lakes during most of the 1800s. There was also a plentiful supply of fuel for these boats. Wood, such as oak and maple that was often used to fire the steamers' boilers was readily available in the towns and villages along the Great Lakes. There was telegraph service in Alcona at the time of the *Marine City* service to the town. This enabled news to be communicated to Bay City and then to Detroit and Toledo newspapers using single transmission on the sole telegraph line. Single transmission was a very slow process, however, and one would have to wait for the line to clear before sending. However, stories

---

[169] "Prosper Times for the Late Marine" originally published in 1910.
* Propeller driven ships as distinguished from side wheeler paddle steamships.
[170] *Shingle Shavers and Berry Pickers,* Oliver Raymond

of this remote area were carried in eastern newspapers, primarily from correspondence by the steamers. In addition to providing a method of communication to the "outside world," steamers also provided a means of getting cash crops, such as barreled fish, apples, berries and hay, and milled lumber to the markets in Detroit.[171] Detroit was a big consumer of hay for virtually all modes of transportation in the city utilized horses. Apple Evaporators* were built and used in many small port towns in order to process apple crops prior to shipping on the steamers. In addition to the crops, ashes were also routinely packed in cases and sold to be used in the tanning business. Also, Canadian hemlocks were harvested for their bark that was used extensively for tanning of leather. Very few Canadian hemlocks now exist in northern Michigan forests as a result.

Salt was another principle article of

---

[171] During the 1880s tobacco products were the most valuable items produced in Detroit's factories. Tobacco was not grown in Michigan, but more chewing tobacco was processed in Detroit than anywhere else in the nation. The climate and methods of production, in addition to the city's reputation as an open shop (a place where employers paid workers at market wages) helped explain this success. The tobacco manufacturers in Detroit produced 40 million cigars annually and Detroit was dubbed the "Tampa of the North." Stoves were another of Detroit's main manufacturing concerns.
Three big companies, the Detroit, Michigan and Peninsular Stove companies, along with other smaller firms, made the city the world's leading producer of iron stoves in the 1880s.The Michigan Stove Company employed 1,200 workers who made more than 76,000 Garland brand stoves each year. During the 1890s, Detroit was also the leading manufacturer of railroad cars. Railroad cars had been made in Detroit since before the Civil War.
Michigan's Past, Michigan History Magazine and overview for teachers.
* Apple Evaporators were used to dehydrate apples cut into slices for preservation and easy shipment

commerce. The years from 1680 to the War of 1812 saw 15,000 to 18,000 barrels of salt hauled over the portage and into the Great Lakes basin from Onondaga Salt mines located in New York. It was headed to Pittsburgh. [172] Salt mining in Michigan began later in 1850. By the 1880s, Michigan salt accounted for 40 percent of the nation's salt production! Many wells were installed with a depth of 600 feet in Saginaw, and extracted salt brine was boiled down for salt. The State of Michigan owned many of the wells. A salt mine was opened beneath the City of Detroit in the year 1910. There is still an estimated 70 trillion tons of un-mined salt still beneath the City of Detroit. [173]

By the years 1833-1834, the fur trade of the upper Great Lakes had reached enormous proportions. During those years, the aggregate business amounted to: 93,168 beaver skins, 694,092 muskrat pelts, 1,069 badger pelts, 7,451 bear pelts, 491 ermine pelts, 9,937 fox pelts, 14,255 lynx pelts, 64,490 sable, 25,100 pole cat pelts, 22,303 otters, 703 raccoon pelts, 8,484 wolf pelts and 1,571 wolverines. [174]

---

[172] "Early Days of Steam Navigation" originally published in 1910

[173] In a related matter, in the 1890s Henry Herbert Dow developed a process for extracting bromine chemicals from brine that he mined from wells in the Midland, Mich. area. These efforts led to the organization of Dow Chemical Company. *"Introducing Michigan's Past," Michigan History Magazine and overview for teachers.*

[174] The source for this is the Hudson Bay Company Business, "Early Days of Steam Navigation," originally published in 1910.

During the fall season on Lake Huron, there was routinely a "herring run." Herring is a fine eating fish with a delicate bone structure. The fish were caught, salted and packed in small barrels. It was considered the last freight of the season and a very valuable cash crop in high demand in ports like Detroit.

During a storm, Lake Huron was a threatening place for lake vessels. In the great storm of September 29 - 30, 1872, 24 steamers and 67 sailing craft were lost on Lake Huron[175] including the well known *Neshoto* with her crew perishing off Sturgeon Point just south of Alcona (see figure 6, pages 80-81).[176] The *Neshoto* was a substantial twin-masted sailing vessel carrying iron ore southbound from Lake Superior to be used in stove manufacturing in Detroit. While apparently trying to make safety in the protective cove of Alcona, she slammed into Sturgeon Point with its newly built Sturgeon Point Lighthouse in the middle of the stormy night. The Captain and the Wheelman floated free on the black cabin deck which came off the wreck and landed on shore while the other five crewmen drowned. A year later only one body came ashore from those who had drowned.[177] An earlier storm on Lake Huron on September 16-19, 1869 claimed 97

---

[175] *Shingle Shavers and Berry Pickers*, Oliver Raymond, p. 68.

[176] A painting by Robert McGreevy of this ship hangs in the Sturgeon Point Museum in Alcona County, Michigan. (See pages 80-81 for copy of print.)

[177] Swenson, Helen. *Sturgeon Point Coast Guard Station*. Central Michigan University, 1967; Clarke Historical Library, Mount Pleasant, Michigan

vessels with a tremendous loss of life.

In 1880, the *Marine City* unloaded the first locomotive from Philadelphia at the town of Alcona, using the larger and sturdier dock facilities with railroad track running the full length of the dock. Docks were moneymakers and returned very well on original investments. Companies often formed corporations with shareholders who contributed their labor instead of cash to capitalize the stock to build docks.[178]

Most of the steamships servicing the coast could not even be considered comfortable. However, the *Marine City* was considered a comfortable passenger vessel in its time. Private cabins, a lounge, and a dining facility that could serve more than 100 at one seating (china dinner service was also included) were available. Dinner, costing 15 to 25 cents, could include fresh fish (usually herring, sturgeon, perch or fried fish eggs), boiled potatoes, canned bread pudding or some other canned delicacy as refrigeration was unavailable. To quench one's thirst for spirits, one had the choice of warm wine, beer, whiskey, scotch or brandy at a small extra cost.

The *Marine City* was not only a passenger vessel. She also transported "package freight" which earlier manifests recorded as hardware, logging chains,

---

[178] Sterling, Elrita M. *First Fifty Years of Harrisville.* Central Michigan University, 1967; Clarke Historical Library, Mount Pleasant, Michigan.

whiskey, shingles, food products, canned goods and, significantly, a number of daguerreotypes or tintype photographs in sealed moisture-proof containers. This method of transporting photographs was common for it insured the protection of the images. These pictures may have been of people in the mines, lumber camps, and villages to the north, all bound to Detroit for further processing or handling. The manifests also included Jewels Jergensen and Elgin pocket watches, that were for sale in these small isolated towns, cases of Bunnahabin Scotch, Dewars Scotch Whiskey and small barrels of ordinary bulk whiskey.[179] A safe for valuables was on board as well. It was a purser's or Express Agent's safe of approximately 36" to 48" high, 24" to 30" wide and about 20" deep with a single combination lock.[180] Insurance records show that this safe was never reported recovered after the steamship's fatal voyage.

---

[179] Unsubstantiated on the trip that resulted in the loss of the *Marine City* – The Actual manifest has not been found. It probably burned with the ship. Based on known common cargo service of period. The *Marine City* was known to be carrying many full barrels of whiskey topside on occasion of its sinking.. See previous footnote.
[180] Common safe for time period. Detroit Post and Tribune, September 3, 1880.

MICHIGAN OPENS TO IMMIGRATION
THE ERIE CANAL
1825

The Erie Canal as originally dug was 40 feet wide at the surface and 28 feet wide on the bottom. The water depth was four feet and it could accommodate boats of 80 to 100 tons burden with shallow drafts.[181] At the time of its completion it was the longest canal in the world, at 363 miles long.[182] Near its completion records list a ship heading across the canal into Lake Erie and then north with cargo consisting of 91 barrels of flour, 101 barrels of whiskey, 63 barrels of pork, 51 barrels of dried fruit, 24 barrels of cider and 16 barrels of beef.[183]

The following is the account of one traveler on the Erie Canal.

> It was our fortune to secure passage on the first boat going west on the canal which is owned by Captain Howell. It was a curiosity for me to ride on such a conveyance as I had not done so before. After riding sometime at that slow rate which such boats are noted for it gradually grew very disagreeable, and I, at last, became completely disgusted as I was confident that I could walk more rapidly myself. Soon, however, we were given a cause for

---

[181] "Early Days of Steam Navigation" originally published in 1910.
[182] http://en.wikipedia.org/wiki/Erie_Cama;
[183] "Early Days of Steam Navigation" originally published in 1910.

greater complaint for as we moved on the canal, a report reached us that there was ice ahead, and that it would be several hours before it would be cleared so that we could reach Buffalo. In the morning, we were recommended to the ship Daniel Webster by a friend to cross Lake Erie. He said it was the best boat and the safest one on the lake. Complying with his recommendation we boarded it but were surprised to behold the most obnoxious place I have ever witnessed. It was filled with foreigners of every description, and fairly alive with the "dregs of humanity," whose indulgence in tobacco and liquors fought the air with an odor too vile to be described by the human language. After sometime we were informed that we could not leave that day, and it was thought not that week in consequence of the lake being iced up. Day after day we waited the time of our departure but the ice prevented our progress.[184]

Charles Dickens provided this description of the canal boat in his book *American Notes for General Circulation*.

On a canal boat, at approximately eight o'clock, the sleeping shelves being taken down and put away and the tables joined together, every body sat down to breakfast which consisted of

---

[184] *Birchbark Belles. Women on the Michigan Frontier*, edited by Larry B. Massie, The Priscilla Press, Allegan Forest, Michigan, 1993.

tea, coffee, bread, butter, salmon, liver, steak, potatoes, pickles, ham, chops, black-puddings, and sausage. When everything was cleared away one of the waiters appeared anew in the character of a barber, shaved such of the company as desired to be shaved while the remainder looked on or yawned over the newspapers. Dinner (midday meal) was breakfast again, without the tea and coffee; and supper (at the end of the day) was dinner and breakfast again with identical fare.[185]

Once the Erie Canal opened, immigration and commerce up through the Great Lakes exploded. Steamships were built to accommodate this demand. One such ship was the *Marine City.*

THE MARINE CITY AND THE TOWN OF ALCONA

Lake Huron is a deep beautiful freshwater sea more than 200 miles north to south and at its widest 183 miles across, including Georgian Bay in Canada. Along its northwestern shore sits a natural protective cove. Situated in this cove, the town of Alcona soon grew into a thriving vibrant village of approximately 1000-1400 year round residents.

August 29, 1880 was a picturesque day for the townsfolk of Alcona, though it was

---

[185] Dickens, Charles. *American Notes for General Circulation*

116

beset with ominous easterly gusts. The sky was blue and the air was fresh and still warm with the scent of the large great white pine trees along the coast. There was evidence of massive lumber cutting as huge clearings of swaths of giant trees along the shore were the most easily harvested and cut. The pine aroma was evident and pleasant. The sun highlighted the cresting waves and crystal clear waters of Lake Huron off the Village of Alcona. The tall white pines along the beach swayed ever-gracefully to the wind's demands. On this beautiful August day, seven steamers and fourteen schooners passed by the Sturgeon Point Lighthouse and were dutifully recorded in the lighthouse log. The southbound *Marine City* had arrived early and was taking on passengers and freight, mostly cedar shingles and cord wood to fuel the ship's substantial boiler. Three stowaways snuck aboard along with about eight new passengers.

The stowaways were from the steamer George Dunlap which was continuing northbound. They had been deckhands that sought free passage to Detroit.

At about 2:30 P.M., the southbound *Marine City* departed the long pier of Alcona with a total of approximately 150 aboard and was soon offshore some three miles to the southeast.

On its fateful trip, the *Marine City* had an estimated 43 first-class passengers on board. Passengers were often accommodated in the same private room with someone they did not know of the same sex.[186] These people undoubtedly had means and property, some of which would have been carried below deck in the hull. There is some speculation that on board was a Sacristy silver chalice, cross and a set of silver collection plates. These items were sent from Father Marquette's church at St. Ignace[187] to be enshrined at the newly built St. Anne's Cathedral in Detroit, the new center of the Catholic Church in the Midwest.[188]

---

[186] Bay City Courier, September, 1880

[187] Point St. Ignace began as a Jesuit Mission in 1607. It became an established white settlement about the time that St. Augustine in Florida was founded and a year before the founding of Jamestown Va. *Birchbark Bells, Women on the Michigan Frontier,* edited by Larry B. Massie, The Priscilla Press, Allegan Forest, Michigan, 1993.

[188] No manifest has been found confirming this. It may not have been listed in any event but placed with someone trustworthy. Stories of Father Marquette's chalice were a legend at the time. Legends of the historical gilded silver chalice of noted American Missionary Explorer Father Jacques Marquette abounded in Northern Michigan. However, it was found in 1912 in the Upper Peninsula under interesting circumstance as recorded by Father Arthur Tonne in "Talks on the Sacramentals." "Back in 1912, there were labor troubles in the Upper Peninsula of Michigan. The National Guard was called to control the situation. Chaplain of the Guard was Monsignor Dunigan, who said Mass daily for the Catholic soldiers.
One morning he noticed two elderly Indians in the back row close to the wall. Next morning they were still closer. They never took their eyes off the priest. Finally they came to the sacristy after Mass and asked if Monsignor Dunigan was the same kind of priest as the fathers who had come to the Indians long ago. Was his Church the same Church as theirs? When he assured them that he was the same kind of priest, they asked him to go with them alone into the woods. They had a treasure which they wanted to turn over to him.
They stopped under a large tree, as one Indian explained that many years before Father Marquette had to leave them to go to an unfriendly group of Indians. Before leaving he called the elders of the tribe and entrusted to them his chalice, which was in a case of cypress wood. If he returned, well and good. If not, they were to guard it with their lives until they could hand it over to some father of his Church.

Shortly after 3:00 PM, this quaint scene was marred by heavy smoke coming from the *Marine City*. She was ablaze about three miles off shore.

The *Marine City* was carrying deck freight of wooden shingles, cedar and pine railroad ties, cedar posts and whiskey in barrels. Some have speculated that the deck cargo promoted conditions optimal for the spread of fire from her normal cinder-laden smoke as she got up steam to disembark. It was also speculated that "coal gas" caused the fire. However, according to statements taken of Captain Comer, the *Marine City* put on wood for fuel at Alcona. So the steamer was likely using mostly wood for fuel southbound.[189] First Mate William Smith was

---

The heroic missionary did not return. That was in 1675. For the next 237 years those Indians kept their treasure The chief would appoint three trustworthy men who alone would know where the chalice was buried. When one died, the chief appointed another three, who would hide it anew. Thus, the chalice was kept for over two centuries. Monsignor Dunigan gladly took charge of the precious treasure. " Talks on the Sacramentals, Father Arthur Tonne, Didde Printing Company, 1950 (www.etwn.com/library/LITURGY/TLKSAC.TXT)
The chalice was restored to the Catholic Church because of the faithful respect of the Indians. It was, in fact, used by Pope John Paul II at the 1999 Papal Mass. (www.silversmithing.com/memnews.htm)

[189] One of the crew was asked by a Detroit Free Press reporter how he thought the fires started. He thought that the fires started because the wood, about 22 to 24 cords, was piled in the dark bunkers on each side and on the front of the boiler and up to the boiler deck. Two lamps were used in the bunkers by the wood passers. Sparks from the fire hole or the lamps might have caused the fire, but whether they did he could not say. The rapid spread of the flames was due to the flammable state of the cargo which was made up of many cords of cedar posts piled on each side of the gangways on the main deck, railroad ties of pine and cedar, piled in the forward and after holds, 50,000 shingles, 30,000 lathe, 160 barrels of fish, 20 whisky barrels, and a number of beer kegs. At the Alcona dock, 8 cords of wood had also been put onboard.

in command of the Steamer. Captain Comer had retired for his usual afternoon nap shortly before.

In very little time, smoke and flame erupted on the hurricane deck. First Mate Smith was immediately alerted to the danger. Not wanting to panic the passengers Smith did not sound the alarm, but he hastened to wake the Captain. Captain Comer, without stopping to dress, rushed forward in his "sleeping clothes" to fight the flames. He began to issue orders from the forward deck to try and contain the fire being fanned by fresh easterly winds. He also ordered the *Marine City* to come about and head full speed towards shore in a north westerly direction to avoid the reefs and rocks of Sturgeon Point.

E.L. Stephenson of Cincinnati said he and three crew members were swapping stories on the main deck when he discovered the fire in the "coal" bunker right below their feet. The men pulled out the fire hoses but when they attempted to charge the line, they discovered that the water valves were rusted shut. The crew also attempted to control the now raging fire with the Steamer's extensive fire fighting apparatus that included 400 feet of hose with multiple "pony engine" steam

---

The lower deck midship was filled full of cedar posts, the kinds used for paving purposes in Detroit. A gangway was kept clear along the starboard side by which passengers could pass back and forth on the main deck. Detroit Free Press, 1880.

driven water pumps. Unfortunately, the crew was not practiced in their use and was unable to act effectively.[190] The fire continued to spread.

The account of E.L. Stephenson of Cincinnati, relates the following in an unedited statement:

> They were leaving Alcona and three of the crew, including him, were sitting on a whiskey barrel on the main deck forward listening to a story of one of the men. The rest of the crew were turning in to repose in the mess room. A new wood passer, who came aboard at Point St. Ignace, and the firemen, suddenly came up on the main deck and said there was a fire in the starboard bunker. A messmate, Steven Welsh, lifted up a hatch and we all saw the flames which swept along the smokestack above. Welsh then ran to Mate Smith and informed him of the fire. The rest of us took down the hose and adjusted it to the pony. Welsh and the Second Engineer Winship then took hold of the hose when it was discovered it had no nozzle and they could throw no stream with force. They called for a nozzle but not obtaining one they ran the hose into the bunker. Winship, the Second Engineer, then tried to turn on the midships steam fire extinguisher, but it would not turn. Neither

---

[190] The Captain and his First Mate would eventually have their U.S. Ship's licenses suspended for this negligence at an official inquest.
Captain Comer was born on October 4, 1847 in Rochester, NY and came to the Great Lakes at the age of two. He sailed the Great Lakes longer than any other man. He started as a deck sweeper at the age of 14 on the Steamer Wisconsin. Then he became a Porter, then Wheelman, and a Captain in 1861. He died penniless in the early 1900s at the Marine Hospital in Detroit.
Shingle Shavers and Berry Pickers, by Oliver Raymond

would the starboard or port extinguisher work. Winship exclaimed, "My God, you couldn't turn those with a crowbar!" Then we rushed up on deck and got the pails. We were cautioned by the First Mate, Mr. Smith, not to give any alarm as it would excite the passengers, but the second cook, when he got on the upper deck yelled, "This man's ship am burning! Lord have mercy on all of them!" This startled the passengers who came rushing out of the cabin. Then I and the crew went forward where we found the Captain, Second Mate and Watchman were in their rooms asleep. The First Mate, Smith, who was on watch, ordered us to go up to the upper deck and throw water on the smoke stack so it would run down on the boiler deck while he awoke the officers. Captain Comer soon appeared and said, "You cannot do any good with the buckets. Lower the boats!" The three of us went forward, the remainder went aft to lower the boats. I then heard the Captain tell the passengers where the life preservers were. I stayed with the Captain and his youngest son, John. The Captain asked me if I had seen his other son, Fred. I told him no. I then took a stool under each arm and jumped from the railing and swam to the *Vulcan*'s yawl boat. I staid (sic) in the boat and made four trips to the burning steamer. On the first trip we picked up Luke Doney, second mate. He staid in the stern of the boat and manned it while we were rowing toward the fire. On our third trip we picked up our clerk, McIntosh, and a man under the rudder; he was dead. We also took two ladies and a little girl off the after wheel fender. On the fourth trip we picked up several women and a man who was on the rudder and had a life - preserver and a big

122

green bench in his arms. He wouldn't let go at first, so we just poked him off with a pike pole. He persisted in hanging on to the bench, and we had to tow him alongside the boat until we reached the *Vulcan*. He was worse to handle than any of the women we picked up. After that trip I went down in the fire-hold of the tug, being exhausted and chilled through. I afterwards went on deck and helped to haul in a person they called Ciney. He had hold of one of the lines thrown out by the *Vulcan*. I was afterward transferred to the tug Grayling and by her taken to Alcona. We were all treated well at the Alcona House. I lost all the clothing I had except a pair of pants and a shirt I had on. On the Metropolis we were ordered down below and were furnished with very little food. On our arrival at Detroit Monday night we had expected to meet the owners of the boat, but were left to find our own lodging and meals. Having had but little to eat since we left Alcona, we were very hungry as well as tired, but we had no money to satisfy our wants. Several of us went down to the foot of First Street and slept on Bissell's truck and barrel staves piled on the dock. Tuesday we had to wait until 3 o'clock before we could get our pay and satisfy our wants. I got the same as the rest, $4.07 for this trip, which is at the rate of $90 per month. I bought a coat and some supper, and now have thirty-five cents, with which I can get a night's lodging and a breakfast in the morning.[191]

The next unedited statement comes from Mrs. H.M. Barker of Jackson:

---

[191] Detroit Free Press, Wednesday, September 1, 1880

123

I had been spending the summer at Mullet Lake House near Cheboygan, at which point I took passage on the steamer *Marine City* to return home. The staterooms were all occupied by one or more, and I was introduced by the steward to my room mate, Miss Sadie Van Arsdale of Cheboygan, who was going to Kalamazoo to attend school. At the time of the disaster I was sitting outside on the after-deck watching the shore as the boat left Alcona. Miss Van Arsdale was reading in the main cabin. Suddenly a little eight-year old boy of Mrs. Moore's rushed on deck screaming as though frightened out of his wits. He was unable to speak, and I thought the child had gone raving crazy. In a moment all the ladies and children in the after part of the boat rushed out of the cabin doors screaming "Fire!" and shrieking at the top of their voices with fear. My first thought was to find my lady friend which I fortunately did in a few seconds among the crowd in the cabin. I had the key of the stateroom in my pocket; together we went to the room; and taking the life preservers, which we found without trouble from under the berths, put them on. A young gentleman adjusted the life-preserver properly on Miss Van Arsdale and then endeavored to fix mine, but by this time had become so nervous and overcome by the terrible excitement that he was unable to help me and I got it on too loose, as I afterwards found out. We then went out on the deck and stood by the railing, but on which side I do not remember. I said to her, "My dear, we must keep together or we'll be lost. You at least must be saved for your parents' sake." By this time fire and smoke issued from the cabin doors and rapidly

124

advanced upon the crying, screaming, shrieking women and children. I never saw such a scene in my life. One little boy fainted from fright, and on all sides the most terrible confusion prevailed. We did not see any officers of the boat, though I have since learned they were shut out by the flames from the stern. As the flames advanced we were pursued by those in front until we were directly over the rudder. The smoke commenced to choke us, and those nearest the flames screamed to us and other near the railing to jump off, so they could get away from the fire. None of us saw the approaching tug *Vulcan*. We were compelled, as we believed to make a choice between death by fire or drowning. I said to Miss Van Arsdale, "jump!" and we both did so together, and when we struck the water found a small cot-bedstead floating near the rudder. It had no doubt been thrown over by some one. She caught hold of one side, I of the other, and we floated away from the steamer about a mile. Owing to its poor adjustment, my life preserver gave me but slight support, and the waves frequently went over me. My right arm is lame, and I was compelled to trust to my left arm entirely for support. Miss Van Arsdale, who is the bravest girl I ever met, never lost her presence of mind, but frequently called to the small boats which we saw in the distance picking up those who had floated away. They seemed to look toward us, but failed to hear or see us and would turn about. I thought I would choke from the water which got into my mouth, and I swallowed a great deal of it. We must have been in the water over an hour, for they told us we were the last ones picked up. A large boat, the life crew's boat, I think, finally came to us, and we were dragged on board limp and helpless. My limbs seemed paralyzed, and in three minutes more, I am sure, I should have been unable to hold to the cot and would have drowned. When they got me in the boat I was laid across the body of a dead man and was powerless to move myself off him. [It has since transpired that the supposed dead man was Mr. S.H. Davis, who was picked up a few moments before, insensible and just letting go his hold of a stateroom door. He was afterward restored to consciousness, and now lies very ill at his home on Brush Street, near Harriet.] They took us on board the tug Graying, and then I lost consciousness. Mr. McDougal, Alpena, and another gentleman on the tug, worked over me until my senses were restored. They took us to Alcona where Miss Van Arsdale and myself were conveyed to the residence of Mr. James Dayton. They sent for Dr. Stockwell, dried our clothes, and did everything possible for our comfort. Miss Van Arsdale took the steamer St. Paul to Cheboygan, and Dr. Stockwell accompanied me on the Steamship Metropolis to Bay City. The officers of the Metropolis were very kind, and attentive, and Mrs. Pierce, wife of the first mate, treated me like a sister. I lost everything I had with me, my trunks containing winter and summer clothing and all my papers.[192]

The most insightful statement comes from Joseph B. Young of Cheboygan, an old barge captain.

I was the last man rescued from the vessel.

---

[192] Bay City Newspaper, possibly The Evening Press.

The fire caught from a lamp kept in the hold by it striking against the side of the boat as related to me by the fireman. When I first saw the fire I called out to the Captain to run the boat ashore, but he refused, saying that he could put the fire out in a few minutes and he started down to fix the hose on the pumps. The engineer, however, had started the pumps, and it was impossible to get the hose attached. Then the captain returned and ordered the boat thrown up in the wind instead of running her to the shore. Had he headed her for the shore, the wind being off the lake, it would have had the effect of throwing the fire forward, off the passengers who were huddled together aft, but as she came up in the wind, the fire swept aft, driving the passengers over the rail into the water. The boats were then lowered, but through some carelessness one of them went down and filled with water almost immediately. Four or five persons who had jumped overboard were lost or clinging to the line from the steamer to the boat, the motion of the former drawing them under water. The other boat was filled with men, while helpless women were struggling in the water. I ran into a stateroom and returned with three or four life-preservers which I handed to some of the passengers. Then I ran up on the upper deck and untied the foot rope of the fender, letting it fall into the water, at the same time sliding down into the water myself.......... The captain's orders were to lower away the boats and get the women into them. Only two boats were lowered and one of them filled. The others were on fire before they could be lowered. Most of the life preservers were rotten and unfit for service. [193]

High winds fanned the flames on the highly flammable painted wooden structure of the boat and its wooden cargo. By this time, word of the fire had reached every passenger on the ship, and the panicked crowd surged upon the upper decks. Pandemonium ensued. Terror-stricken men, women and children massed at the fore and aft to avoid the advancing flames. Many fled over the railing, leaping into the water below. Women were particularly vulnerable since clothing of the period did not promote staying afloat with water-logged long skirts.

The fire enveloped the zinc lined engine room, forcing the crew to seek refuge on the upper decks. The steering wheel and helm were engulfed in the flames. The *Marine City* lost momentum, ran out of steam, and drifted helplessly approximately one mile from the shore north of Sturgeon Point. Passengers continued jumping overboard. Many men, some burned about their heads, arms, and hands, risked their lives to help women, children and the elderly into the rough waters. Others helped floundering passengers to floating loose doors, boards or tables. Miraculously one girl was saved by the air trapped beneath her wide skirts and petticoats that buoyed her up. One woman

---

[193] Detroit Free Press, Wednesday, September 1, 1880

was lost overboard and drowned after having just given birth on the main deck in front of the clerk's office. No confirmable record can be found of the newborn infant, but at least one source said that the newborn child died.

The billowing smoke was visible for miles. This was the sole good fortune of the *Marine City*. The tugboat *"Vulcan"* was a mile from the burning steamer. Without delay, Captain Thomas Hackett steered his boat toward the disaster. With tremendous foresight, Captain Hackett had all life boats manned and all other preparations for rescue were made while en route. His crew was well practiced, well disciplined by all accounts, and ably directed by a firm Captain. The *Vulcan* ran up along side the *Marine City*, catching fire herself in the process. The crew of the tug promptly extinguished the fires on the upper decks of the tug with high pressure water hoses driven by the *Vulcan*'s fully operational steam pumps. Others pulled survivors out of the choppy waters and off the flaming wreck and onto the tug.[194] Two of the high pressure hoses that were used by the *Vulcan* were employed to control the fire behind the numerous passengers as they tried

---

[194] Captain Thomas Hackett was awarded a jeweled and engraved solid gold medal with a relief of a burning *Marine City* and the tug Vulcan speeding to her rescue in commemoration of his deeds by the citizens of Detroit. (See last page of this publication.) He and Engineer McCabe were also awarded gold watches by a wealthy brewer, E.W. Voight. Mr. Voight and his wife were among the rescued passengers. July 1958, Telescope, Great Lakes Marine Institute.

to disembark onto the *Vulcan*. A third hose was aimed at the *Vulcan* herself to keep her from catching fire.[195]

The Life Saving Crew, based out of Sturgeon Point Lighthouse about a mile away, arrived in a surfboat later and rescued some passengers. (See page 86, Figure 9, for painting of the crew of another life saving boat.) They would have arrived earlier if they had not been out blackberry picking.[196] They rushed back to their post and launched their surfboat when the remaining lookout at the Lighthouse raised the alarm. Two months later Captain Percy Silverthorne of the Sturgeon Point Life Saving Crew was to resign his command due to harsh disapproval of the delay and his lax management of the life saving station.

There was much criticism of the lifesaving station at Sturgeon Point. It apparently was an utter failure during this disaster. Some witnesses state that at the time, Captain Silverthorne was at his farm two miles away where reports say he remains too much for the good of the Service, and two of the remaining six men were out gathering berries. Captain Silverthorne claimed to have had four men on duty but no one saw more

---

[195] Swenson, Helen. *Sturgeon Point Coast Guard Station.* Central Michigan University, 1967; Clarke Historical Library, Mount Pleasant, Michigan
[196] This was allowed by the U.S. Lighthouse Rules to augment food sources. Gardening was allowed as well in this isolated wilderness, and the Lighthouse had an extensive vegetable garden. "Michigan Lighthouses: an aerial photographic perspective" John L Wagner, 1994.

than two at work and these were not of any conspicuous service. While the Life Saving Station crew was a mile to a mile and a half nearer the burning Steamer than the row boats on the shore of Alcona, the latter reached the stricken vessel much sooner and did vastly greater service. A newspaper reported that there was a very general complaint against Captain Silverthorne, and no doubt is expressed that he and his crew are quite a useless expense to the government. It was reported that he had none of the qualities which fit him for the position. The account goes on to say that "he is a slow motion, farmer-like man with no special sailor training and no qualities fit him for action in any emergency. He does not train his crew, and, in short, does little beyond drawing his salary. The "keeper of the light" at Sturgeon Point is regarded by the mariners and citizens of the shore as vastly more fit name for the man for the place." Another quoted critic stated, "One thing seems to be certain, not only at this station, but of all others and that is that the Lifesaving Service needs remodeling on a different basis. Now the crews are made up of men hired by the month for the season of navigation. In the winter they work in lumber camps and wherever else they can find employment. The proper way would seem to be to place the service in the hands of the Navy, enlist sailors regularly into it and train them as members of the single service are trained."[197]

Other small boats were deployed from Alcona led by Commodore William Hill to aid the stricken vessel. He and his fellow town-folks saved a number of lives. These small able boats were manned by Charles Fleck, Ford Smith, Barney Hill, George Allen, Fred Card and James Donahoe, all residents of Alcona.

The tugboat "Grayling" was coming out of Black River five miles to the north towing a raft of logs when its crew saw the towering pillar of smoke of the burning *Marine City*. Her tow was quickly cut loose and the tug sped to help.[198] She arrived 45 minutes after the fire began, doing in excess of ten miles per hour, her top speed. The Grayling and her crew rendered all assistance that was possible, also rescuing crew and passengers from the rough water.

The captains and crews of both tugs worked in tandem, pulling many to safety. Few could swim and even, with life preservers, they were floundering in the high waves cast about by the strong easterly winds.

Upon returning to shore, the Alcona community welcomed and comforted

---

[197] From the The Detroit Post and Tribune, Tuesday, morning, September 7, 1880.
[198] This was no small feat. A tow was worth thousands of dollars and could mean the loss or a fortune for the captain and crew.

survivors, many of whom were severely burned, opening their homes and rendering what first aid they could in this remote isolated northern village. The following is an excerpt of a letter written by the editor of the newspaper The Toledo Blade, Mr. John McElroy, who lost his father-in-law and son in the disaster. The letter was written from Detroit to his paper. Mrs. McElroy was on the *Marine City* with her father, Dr. Pomeroy, and her son. She was rescued, but her father and her son drowned. Mr. McElroy writes:

But whatever their surrounding, the people of Alcona, one and all, bear that stamp of genuine nobility, which nature frequently delights in setting upon even the humblest. They have that grandest of nobilities, where

> *Kind hearts are more than coronets*
> *And simple faith in Norman blood*

Certainly there never was a community in which everybody bore the test of a great emergency more admirably and which had absolutely no one that did not do more than his whole duty. In all the 130 survivors of the disaster there is not one breath of complaint against any man, woman or child in Alcona but on the other hand enthusiastic laudation of everybody and all they did. I challenge duplication of this anywhere in the world. How Alcona escaped having at least one mean man, anxious to make merchandise of the miseries of others is a secret I wish she would communicate to other places. If her pine industries bring about this blessed result, then let us all pave our streets with sawdust, and perfume the air with the resiny odors arising from piles of lumber, lath and piny refuse.

At the first site of flames rising from the *Marine City*, the only two boats on the beach were hastily manned and rowed as rapidly as strong muscles, keyed up with intense excitement, could do it. These did superb service in picking up the people in the water, and as fast as the rescued were landed, either from these boats or the tugs *Vulcan* or Grayling, the people of the town took them in hand. Those who had been in the water were undressed, rubbed, and clothed again in dry garments furnished by their benefactors, who in some instances almost stripped themselves to do this. Thousands of dollars were taken from the dripping pockets, dried, and returned without the loss of a cent by anyone. Remember that this was done by people who think $30 a month good wages and $40 almost affluence and from whole gifts of clothing, etc, meant the donation of weeks of hard toil with the ax or handspike.[199]

The Steamer Metropolis left nearby Alpena the next day upon hearing of the tragedy for Alcona to give aid. It would eventually transport survivors and injured to their homeports.

Though it is impossible to know the exact lives lost, due to the fact that the passenger records burned with the ship, the best estimate of the clerk, steward and

---

[199] The Detroit Post and Tribune, Tuesday Morning, September 7, 1880.

134

surviving passengers sets the number close to 20. Some of the dead were women. Most of the bodies recovered were initially buried in the Harrisville Cemetery. Some relatives of the deceased came from great distances to disinter their loved ones bodies and take them home.

The most complete known list of the dead are as follows: Richard Schultz; James Wilkins; Musician Frank Emmett of Port Huron; John McElroy of Toledo; a man with the last name of Duncan; James Pomeroy of Ottawa, Ohio; Ed Ray; Head Cook James Parsons; Miss Jeannie Musser of Alcona; a person by the last name of Foster of Detroit; an Irishman by the name of McKerren or McKarren of Detroit; James Griffen of Detroit; Martin J. Lawson of Detroit; an unnamed man of Point St. Ignace and an unidentified woman and a new born babe. Eight positively identified as drowning after jumping overboard are the following: Frank Emmett of Port Huron, Martin T. Watson a Detroit businessman/pharmacist, crewmembers Richard Schultz and James Cook, passengers James Griffen, John McElroy and Dr. Pomeroy all from Toledo, Ohio.

The unfortunate Dr. Pomeroy became wild with excitement and seizing his grandson, little John McElroy, plunged overboard and both drowned. Martin T. Watson, a young druggist who graduated from Pharmaceutical School, known to be an expert swimmer, drowned also when he jumped overboard. Thomas Griflin, another cook on the *Marine City*, ran up and down not knowing what to do and threw himself into the lake. Without making any effort to save himself, he commenced calling upon others for help and eventually became exhausted and perished beneath the waves.

Three days later, on September 2nd, another woman's body was taken from the wreck of the *Marine City* by William L. McDougall, a submarine diver attached to the wrecking Schooner Lilly Amiott. He was searching for the safe belonging to the McClure Express Company that was known to be on the *Marine City*. The safe was never found. The body was so badly burned it could not be recognized. The whole face and front of the body was entirely consumed by the fire.[200] Her remains are believed to be buried at Sturgeon Point with a plain, hand carved wooden cross over her sandy grave. Other sources say she was buried at Mt. Joy cemetery, up the hill behind Alcona or at

---

[200] The Detroit Post and Tribune, Friday morning, September 3, 1880 reported a dispatch from Alcona as follows:

Shocking Discovery: A body supposed to be that of a woman was taken from the wreck of the *Marine City* today by William L. McDougall, a submarine diver attached to the wrecking schooner Lilly Amiott, while in search for the safe belonging to McClure's Express Company. The body is so badly burned as to be UNRECOGNIZABLE. The whole face and front of the body has been entirely consumed. TERRIBLE FOREBODING. Some bones were also found in the hold, indicating that other bodies were consumed. The bones are undoubtedly the remains of the stowaways who were said to have been on the *Marine City*. It is believed that further discoveries will be made tomorrow.

Harrisville. No further record could be found of her.

In addition, some human bones were found in the hold indicating that other bodies were consumed. It is believed these bones belonged to the young stowaways that were known to have been on the *Marine City*.

An inquest was held on the bodies of Martin T. Watson and an unknown man picked up from the wreck of the *Marine City* on the 29th of August 1880. It was a verdict of the Coroner's jury that the deceased came to their deaths by drowning and further the jury returned an opinion that there is no blame to be attached to any of the officers or crew and that everything was done that could have been done to save the lives of those on board. This verdict was signed by L. Boardman, Foreman of the jury and G.W. LaChapelle, Coroner. These bodies were originally interred in Harrisville but friends of the deceased applied for the remains, and they were taken up and removed to Detroit.

A great deal of misinformation about the natural characteristics of the Great Lakes was published in newspapers at the time of the *Marine City* disaster. One paper reported "that the prospects of recovering the bodies is very uncertain because Lake Huron is by far the deepest of the Great Lakes having an average depth exceeding one thousand feet everywhere. Add to this the great expanse of the lake, the continual shifting of the winds, and the almost interminable stretches of sparsely inhabited coast, the chances that the bodies will come ashore where they will be found and recognized becomes dishearteningly small."

Mr. Frank E. Beard, correspondent of the Post and Tribune of Alcona, later telegraphed several additional statements given by a variety of people involved in the shipwreck. It is interesting to note that there was a telegraph in Alcona. The directory for the Village, in fact, shows that Western Union operated out of Alcona at this time. Please note that the grammar and syntax in the following statements are quoted directly from the source without editing.

J.M. Jones was a passenger from Alpena. He was rescued and returned on the Grayling. This is his statement:

> I was standing at the engine room door on the port side talking to another gentleman when I smelled smoke. We looked into the fire room door and there was fire and flames in the starboard bunkers among the wood and coal. I called the attention of the fireman and engineer to the same and efforts were at once made to get a stream of water on the fire. The hose were promptly got on and then went up into the cabin. As I opened the cabin door I found it full of smoke. I immediately gave the alarm that the boat was on fire. The most intense excitement prevailed and regular panic ensued, passengers jumped into the water long before there was any need of doing so. The officers and crew behaved nobly, with the single exception of the second

engineer who acted like an insane man. Boats were lowered as soon as possible and filled at once. [201]

Mr. Jones remained on the boat until he was rescued by the *Vulcan*. He was not able to give any idea as to how many were aboard or how many lives were lost.

Another statement was given by Captain Van Liew of the tug Grayling:

> I was engaged towing a raft abreast of Black River when I first saw the flames around the smokestack of the *Marine City*. The flames were running about as high as the smokestack and the steamer was three miles from Alcona. I let go the raft immediately and went to the rescue. When I reached her she had been on fire about forty-five minutes. The *Vulcan* had been alongside and taken all the passengers off the wreck. I picked up five women and six men. Four of the women had life preservers. One man died before reaching shore. I ran along side the *Vulcan* and took off all I could carry and then landed at Alcona and then went back. Captain Hackett landed a second load. The *Vulcan* was coming up the lake from Tawas and was first along side the *Marine City*. She did splendid taking off all the passengers that were left and was badly scorched on one side, black and charred. When I reached the wreck the lake was full of floating furniture, baggage, etc, and there were from twenty-five to thirty people in the water. The small boats picked up the very last life preserver. The Sturgeon Point lifesaving crew reached the *Marine City* about thirty

---

[201] Post and Tribune of Alcona, 1880, found at www.hhpl.on.ca

minutes after the fire broke out. The wind was from the northwest, blowing fresh, and quite a sea was running. The people at Alcona did everything possible for the passengers. When I left the wreck was still burning. The upperworks were all burned off to the water's edge. She drifted ashore about half way between Alcona and Sturgeon Point, broadside to the beach.[202]

Another passenger, Mrs. A.B. Clough, also gave an account. Mrs. Clough was from Marine City. She was traveling with her son, Burt, and had been visiting R.B. Clough:

I was in my stateroom in the after cabin reading when I heard someone say fire and soon heard it repeated. I thought it was used in conversation. My son Burt came running into the stateroom exclaiming that the boat was on fire. I at once went into the cabin and found it full of smoke. I went aft. Burt was determined to jump overboard but I restrained him. I found a life preserver but before I could get it on a headstrong man, a stranger to me, jerked it away from me. I then found Dr. Stockwell of Alcona and with his kind assistance, Burt and I reached the main deck. I picked up a boy about six years old who had been separated from his parents and was nearly frightened to death. All of us got on the side of the gunwale and held by a window on the porter's room. A line was thrown to us but the Doctor did not catch it and he lost his balance, went overboard and was picked up. We were held in position and were rescued. Burt fainted once from the heat. The

---

[202] Ibid

140

fire spread rapidly and the boat soon burned to the water's edge and sank.

Many of the acts of heroism were rewarded. Following the disaster John Millen, Jr. of Black River was rewarded for his heroic deeds with a gold watch and chain by the Merchant and Manufacturing Exchange of Detroit. Many articles in the Toledo Blade, written by the husband of Mrs. McElroy, celebrated the valiant efforts of all of those who saved lives. Mrs. A.B. Clough received recognition for her heroic actions during the fire when she saved Joseph Voigt, a six year old boy whom she found wandering lost on the burning boat and then put safely in a lifeboat without getting into the over filled lifeboat herself. The grateful parents of Joseph Voigt awarded her a silver tea set. Charles Thorne was the Steward of the *Marine City* who personally saved several lives and had his hands badly burned.

It was reported in the Iosco County Gazette on September 2, 1880 by several witnesses that:

> The terrible story of this disaster will never be fully written, yet the glimpses of it as narrated by many survivors, reveals the sad fact that heroes and cowards travel side by side, and that it but requires such an emergency to develop the utter fiendishness of some human beings. Helpless women with babes in their arms were repeatedly stripped of the life-preservers they had secured, by

strong men who could easily have got others or saved themselves without, while of some it may be truthfully said that "they perished in the effort to save others." Foremost among these should stand the name of Richard Schultz, the head-waiter, who buckled on a fire-extinguisher and deliberately faced the advancing flames, and, pouring on the stream, remained at the post until burned to death[203].

Joseph Mero was a crewmember of the Tug *Vulcan*. He was so badly burned and incapacitated from his efforts to save passengers on the *Marine City* that he later had to support his family by sweeping the floors of the Timkin Detroit Axel Company as he could no longer work on a ship. The *Vulcan* approached the side of the burning Steamer, and Mero, at the risk of his own life, boarded the *Marine City* and dragged passenger after passenger to the Tug kicking in doors and opening blocked passageways by force. Among those he rescued were E.W. Voigt, a well-known wealthy Detroit brewer, Mrs. Voigt, their son and the Voigt family nurse. Even after helping to save the Voigt family, he went on to save several other people from the boat sustaining serious and severe burns about his head and hands and arms. Mr. Voigt presented him with an engraved solid silver watch. The Detroit Merchants and Manufacturers Exchange

---

[203] Iosco County Gazette, September 2, 1880

presented him with a gold and silver medal. Mr. Voigt, realizing the seriousness of this man's injuries, offered him a job at his brewer, but he declined it being a temperate man. He was born in Amherstburg and sailed on the Lake practically all of his life until incapacitated. He finally got a sailing job again several years later working on a Detroit area ferry boat where he fell through an open hatchway and was killed.

Mr. Voight also presented other officers and crew of the *Vulcan* with very valuable gold and silver watches and charms. The watches presented to the officers ranged in value from about $150 to $175, according to rank.[204] Those officers that were presented with a watch included: Thomas Hackett, Captain; Robert H. Sunderland, Mate; Patrick C. McCabe, First Engineer; George B. Kelley, Second Engineer. The following crewmembers received watches: Joseph M. Peltier, Lookout; Daniel Kelley, Wheelsman, Ralph H. Hackett; George Manley; Joseph Dent; Samuel J. Lewis, Steward; Joseph Mearon and George W. Black, Deckhands.[205]

The *Marine City* reportedly burned to the water line and sank shortly afterward relatively close to shore. After the accident, the crew and many of the passengers of the

---

[204] $150 - $175 is equal roughly to $3,131.60 to $3653.53 in 2006. Values determined using inflation calculator found at www.westegg.com/inflation/infl.cgi
[205] Sarnia Observer, September 17, 1830

Marine City were transferred to the Steamer Metropolis the next day which transported them to Bay City.

A crowd of several hundred people at Maxwell's Wharf in Bay City greeted the Metropolis as it came into view. The Evening Press of the Bay City Newspaper reported on August 31, 1880 as follows:

> The crowd of passengers as they came from boat to wharf furnished food for the artist's brush. All were decidedly weather beaten; some were without hats and had handkerchiefs tied over their heads. Others were minus shoes and we heard of a case in which one of the survivors offered $10 for a pair of somewhat worn shoes, so great was the demand. The colors of the passengers ranged from decidedly pallid white to the darkest negro, who was unable to turn white from fear, but according to one he was "scared enough for to die."[206]

In addition to the Metropolis, it was reported in the Western Home Journal of September 4, 1880, that a special train was placed at the disposal of the *Marine City* survivors by the Detroit and Bay City Railroad Company. The train took them to Detroit without further delay or cost. The passengers of the *Marine City* owed their thanks for this kindness to Superintendent Callaway of the railroad who ordered the train put together right away.[207]

---

[206] The Evening Press, Bay City, Tuesday, August 31, 1880
[207] The Western Home Journal, Detroit, Saturday, September 4, 1880

The *Marine City* was insured for a total of $15,000 by the following companies: The Orient Insurance Company for $1,000; Greenwich Insurance Company $2,500; Phoenix Insurance Company $4,000; Toledo Fire and Marine $2,500; Union Insurance Company $2,000; Lamar Insurance Company $1,500; Lloyd's of London $1,500.

Later, several attempts were made to grapple and tow the sunken hull into shallower water to try to salvage the engine, boiler, and personal effects. These were to no avail. With the approaching winter, rough, icy waters prevented effective salvage at such depths. Large amounts of collapsed, burned debris protected the underlying hull compartments. Over the years, the compartments became obscure with shifting sand underneath the burnt timbers. The exact location of the underlying hull remains unknown. However some of the hull and the top metal superstructure and boiler were shoved into shallower water by the winter ice over many seasons.

There is an unsubstantiated rumor that the fire had been set by a jealous lover who was an employee of one of the lumber operations in Alcona. The young woman who was the object of his desire announced she was to marry another. This groom-to-be was said to have been a young man who worked for the Alger Smith Co., which controlled much of the expanding lumber industry in

145

N.E. Michigan. The young woman supposedly embarked on the *Marine City* for Detroit to attend to her wedding plans. This unknown young woman died on the *Marine City* and her body was never identified, nor purportedly was a multi-carat jeweled engagement ring and studded jeweled necklace, a wedding gift, she was reported to have on her person. In the late 1890's Lloyd's of London allegedly paid out a claim to a family for unknown reasons after protracted litigation. Whether this was the fabled lost jewelry or not is unclear. Further archival research was requested of Lloyds of London, England with no confirmation. This story is still uncorroborated.[208] Admiralty Records and Federal Court Records do not reveal any such claims. No one claims to know how, or possibly even why, the fire actually began. The Detroit Post and Tribune, however, took some pains to investigate how the fire started, retaining experts, even in the face of the eye witness allegation that one or more lamps broke in the hold. They concluded that "it was clearly due to spontaneous ignition of gas generated in the coalbunkers. This theory is supported by P.E. Saunders, a member of the local board of Steamboat Inspectors, and David Gallagher, General Agent of the

---

[208] Oral history, Captain Armand Pearson of Alcona Beach, north of Harrisville, Michigan, and Mabel Zimmerman (who was married to a coastguardsman of Sturgeon Point's light house). Actual records have not been produced. The Law Firm of Robert L. Bunting continues to search Admiralty Records and archives.

People's Line. Mr. Saunders says he was thoroughly familiar with the engine room of the *Marine City* and the workings of her machinery and is positive that the fire was not caused by the imperfection of any part of her engine or boiler. Mr. Gallagher states that when the *Marine City* had her boiler cleaned out while in port last week she took on coal. He discovered that coal of a smaller size than had been used heretofore was now being put onboard and challenged Captain Comer about it. The latter went up to the coal dock and gave orders to have the coal of the usual size placed onboard. The small coal which had already been loaded was not removed from the bunkers, and Mr. Gallagher is of the opinion that the gases were generated by this coal. Had not the fire been caused by the ignition of the gas it would not have spread as rapidly as it did.[209]

However, the frequent coats of paint which the Steamer had received during the 14 years she had been afloat doubtless had much to do with facilitating the spread of the devouring element."[210]

There is another myth regarding the *Marine City*. It comes from an article in the September 15th, 1884 edition of the newspaper *Detroit Post*. The author of the article tells of a phantom light that could be seen at midnight on the anniversary of the burning of

---

[209] Bay City Courier, September 1880
[210] Ibid

147

the *Marine City* for many years after. The author went to investigate the light with a local fisherman, and he saw the light "as plain as the stars that twinkled in the heavens."[211] The fisherman voiced a theory about the phantasmal light.

He hypothesized that the *Marine City* was a victim of arson by a crewmember for a wrong, real or imagined grievance. This man was claimed in the flames and waves. The fisherman went on to explain that if this were true, then the arsonist was "doomed as punishment to bring that light here every night during the month in which the boat was lost, to light the others that were lost safely over the 'dark waters,' and possibly as a warning to others that may be like tempted to murder or other wickedness."[212]

In the U.S. District Court, Southern District of Michigan, Eastern Division Detroit, in the general records is found case no. 2513. These Court pleadings are principally in handwritten form and difficult to read. The lawsuit states a company by the name of Michigan Transportation Company was alleged to be the owner of the *Marine City* and filed a petition for Limitation of Liability for losses and claims connected with the burning under

---

[211] Detroit Post, 15 September, 1884.
(www.hhpl.on.ca/GreatLakes/Scripts/News/Article.asp?ID=5743, Contributed by Dave Swayze)
[212] Detroit Post, 15 September, 1884.
(www.hhpl.on.ca/GreatLakes/Scripts/News/Article.asp?ID=5743, Contributed by Dave Swayze)

existing Admiralty Law at the time. In this preceding, $650 dollars was pledged by the company to offset personal property loss and another $650 for loss of life and the injured. This is the value determined by appraisers of such loss of personal baggage and life as the *Marine City* now lies sunk off the coast of Lake Huron according to this proclamation signed by three appraisers. On the 29th day of August 1880, according to Court records, the *Marine City* was bound for Toledo, Ohio. In these Court actions, one interesting case was brought by Elizabeth C. Moore of Ottawa, Ohio. She alleges, through her lawyer's flowery handwritten complaint, that she booked passage for herself and her daughter. She claims a loss of $442.50 for clothing and sundries including jewelry lost in a trunk placed in the hold for which she was given a receipt which was never recovered. A detailed itemized list of the trunks contents reveals silk dresses, lace, umbrella, hats, kid gloves, an all wool walking suit, four ladies underwear and much more. A copy of this inventory is included in the appendix of this book including a listing of 1880's values.

The company answered the lawsuit alleging, "on or about August 29th, 1880, said Steamer being well-manned, appointed and appareled and being in every respect tight, staunch, strong and seaworthy was off Harrisville in said district and bound upon a voyage between Mackinac, Michigan and

Toledo, Ohio. The owner further alleged that the said burning and sinking of the said Steamer and said loss of life and loss and damage of property which resulted therefrom and particularly the loss of any property belonging to Elizabeth C. Moore, Mary M. Baker and other claimants hereinafter mentioned was not caused in whole or in part by the design and neglect of your petitioner but said loss, damage, injury and loss of life and property was occasioned without the design, neglect, fault, privity or knowledge of your petitioner (the boat owner). That said loss nor damage happened through any neglect or failure to comply with the provisions of Title 52 of the revised Statutes of the United States nor through any known defects or imperfections of the steaming apparatus or the hull of said steamer and petitioner claimed the limitations provided in Section 42.83, 42.85 and 42.86 of the revised Statutes of the United States and the rules of this Court. (sic)" There was no record of the results of these Court actions.

In World War II the *Marine City*'s boiler was allegedly salvaged for much needed iron. The remains are now protected by law, which forbids damaging or removing any part of the shipwreck. Some of the iron, wooden beam superstructure and boiler mounts are close to shore. There are rumors that silverware, coins with dates of 1880 and preceding, chains, latches, barrel spigots have been found by locals to this day. One local said, "if one could recover all the artifacts recovered from the wreck of the *Marine City* by the locals along the beach, you could rebuild her." The *Marine City*'s tall rudder washed up on shore 80 years after the incident and is on display at the Sturgeon Point Museum.

A painting of the *Marine City* (see figure 7, pages 82-83) by marine artist and historian Robert McGreevy is now on display at the Sturgeon Point Lighthouse. There has been so much interest in this grand ship that a limited number of lithographic prints of the McGreevy painting were issued and readily sold out amongst collectors and enthusiasts.

One may stroll one mile north of Sturgeon Point Lighthouse along the beach. There, a mere dozen yards from the shoreline appears some of the metal superstructure and significant wooden beams of the *Marine City* still breaching the waves. A ribbed skeletal section of the steamer lays sprawled about this rusted and decaying testament. One can easily succumb to temptation and wade out to this eerie wreck and snorkel it as many still do. Other timbers and structure of the ship are submerged further out. On a clear day one can boat over them and see their ghostly forms lying forever still. It is all that remains of the *Marine City* for much of the hull and its 1880 cargo, despite numerous searches, is lost beneath the eternal shifting sands and waves of Lake Huron.

151

THE GHOST TOWN OF ALCONA

The Bay City Evening Post reported the following:

> The people of Alcona threw open their houses to the sufferers; furnished them with clothing as far as possible; provided food and did everything possible to make the survivors comfortable. The passengers say they owe the Alconians an everlasting debt for their kindness. When the Metropolis left yesterday three cheers were given, for the people of Alcona, with a will, and they were echoed by the Alconians.[213]

Now there is nothing apparent of the town, no pier, no narrow gauge railroad, street or structures.

From the Detroit Post and Tribune, Tuesday Morning, August 31, 1880 we get a list of the saved and the lost:

The Saved, Passengers
Altman, Charles, Alpena
Barker, Mrs. Mary H. Jackson
Barrett, T.H. Pt. St. Ignace
Byron, Nell, Ontario
Bishop, Mary H. Memphis, MI
Beard, F.E., Alcona
Bliss, Mr. and Mrs., Port Huron
Breen, John H., Detroit

---

[213] The Evening Press, Bay City, Tuesday, August 31, 1880.

Brennan, T.B., Detroit
Brewer, Miss Anna, Tecumseh
Brown, C.I., Detroit
Butterfield, G.T. and wife, Alpena
Campbell, Mrs. Eliza, Port Huron
Cary, L.N., Lexington
Clemens, Charles, Toledo
Clough, Mrs. A.B. and son, Marine City
Cole, W.B., Rogers City
Colson, George, Port Huron
Covill, Dewitt, Toronto
Casey, Mr., Detroit
Davis, B.H., Detroit
Doolittle, Mr. and Mrs. George H., Port Huron
Douglass, Fred, St. Clair
Field, Effie, Detroit
Freer, Frank, Detroit
Galling, Charles, and two children, Alpena
Grant, Mrs. and daughter, Grosse Pointe
Gray, Mrs. J., Port Huron
Goodrich, Annie
Heron, John, Alcona
Hobbs, George, Port Huron
Herbard, Katie, Detroit
Howard, Lafayette, Alcona
Hudson, Alice, Alcona
Hueber, Mrs. Charles, Alpena
Jones, J.N., Alpena
Keifer, A., Alcona
Kenoose, T.F., Tecumseh
Keys, John, Alpena
King, W.A., St. Catherines
Laralu, Joseph

Levere, Jules, Alpena
Lumsden, Mrs. W.O. and child, Detroit
Matthews, Ella, Alpena
Miller, Edward, Port Huron
Matthews, Robert, Alpena
Miller, Edward, Port Huron
Matthews, Robert, Alpena
Morris, William, Port Huron
McConnell, Miss J.A., Toledo
McConnell, Miss Margaret, Toledo
McElroy, Mrs. John, Toledo
McGraw, Pat, Pt. St. Ignace
McLenna, Jonas, Harrisville
Miller, Charles, Detroit
Miller, Joseph, Rogers City
Moebe, Gus, Alpena
Moore, Mrs. J.J. and son, Ottawa, Ohio
Mott, Frank, Utica, Mich.
Moore, Frank, Toledo
Newman, C.W., Jr. Detroit
Osmun, Mr. and Mrs. C.A., Greenville
Perrult, Joseph, Alpena
Quinn, Patrick, Cadillac
Ryan, E.J., Toronto
Schumm, C.H., Detroit
Soguer, Isaac, Montreal
Schonk, Charles, Alpena
Seguin, Isaac, Alpena
Sharp, Miss Jenny, Cheboygan
Sharp, Mrs. Lizzie, Cheboygan
Spittle, John, Detroit
Strekwell, Dr. G.A., Alcona
Thompson, Miss Alice, Port Huron

Thompson, Mrs. C.H. and Son, Detroit
Thompson, Lattimer, Toledo
Thompson, Louise, Detroit
Young, J.B.
Van Arsdale, Miss Sadie, Cheboygan
Voight, E.W. and family, Detroit
White, Mr. and Mrs. and four children, Detroit

The Saved, Officers and Crew
Capt. W.E. Comer and two sons
William Smith, mate
Robert McClure, chief engineer
C.A. Winship, second engineer
C.A. McIntosh, clerk
C. Thorn, Steward
Robert McClure, second express agent
Crew - Fred Gibbs, George Shields, Richard M.
Johnson, James Conner, M. Casey, Ed
Stevenson, John Batten, Charles Crocket,
Stephen Walsh, William Hygt, Robert Mott,
James Kinney, Charles Hogues, John Sullivan,
A.W. Enshaw, Alexander Monroe, Geo.
Buchard, Henry Reeds, Herbert Hatch, Joe
Trombley, Frank Sheldrick, Edward Phillips,
Luke Davey, James Goodwin, John Healy,
Thomas Hanley, Charles Hatch, John Curry,
C.A. Smith, James Crawford, Zack Dunn,
Nelson Austin

The Lost
(The following are those listed as missing and
believed to be drowned. The trip sheets of
the *Marine City* which gave the passenger's

155

names were burned, so determining the exact number lost was difficult.)

The father and son of Mrs. McElroy, wife of the editor of the Toledo Blade
Jenny Muzzy of Alcona
Richard Schultz, headwaiter
James Griflin, headcook
Frank Emmett, a musician on the boat, of Port Huron
Nicholas Watson of Detroit
Deck passenger, name not known, from St. Ignace
Lady who jumped overboard and drowned shortly after giving birth to a child on the main deck
Three Unknown stowaways
Badly burned unrecognizable body of a young woman

EPILOGUE

The Detroit Post and Tribune, Tuesday morning, August 31, 1880, carried an article asking why steamers could not be fire proof. The article states that "Once more a grave marine disaster, attended with loss of life, emphasizes the questions: Is it necessary to construct the light woodwork of passenger steamers so as to resemble a shell of tinder, which will burn so rapidly as to afford those on board only a few hurried minutes in which to escape? Is it necessary to so construct passenger steamers that their whole upper works will be consumed in case of fire, in

156

fifteen minutes? Cannot modern invention provide at least measurable fire-proof passenger vessels at a moderate cost? - vessels that, if they burn at all, will burn slowly, affording at least some hours of comparative safety for their passengers, in which to make port or to escape in boats quietly and without panic, saving not only their lives, but also their most valuable portable property."

The article goes on to say that "the way in which boats are usually constructed is an almost direct invitation to fire. Their woodwork is light of the pine - one of the most flammable of woods - and its flammability is increased by putting upon it coat after coat of oil paint. The decks are also of a material which is of the nature of tinder. Once let a fire be started and catch the light painted wood-work and destruction is certain and terribly rapid." The article goes on to state that the "*Marine City* was probably as well provided against fire, and as safe, as most boats of her class. She was constructed like nearly all the rest, and was probably more carefully watched and handled than some others. Her unfortunate ending will naturally tend to injure the general passenger traffic of steamers wherever there are competing lines of railroad. Yet summer travel by boat is certainly the pleasantest and most comfortable mode of traveling, and as a rule, one of the safest. But there is a greater horror of fire at sea than of almost any other known peril to which travelers are exposed. Let this peril be avoided, and travel by steamer lines would be noticeably increased."[214]

No one learned from the *Marine City* disaster and on June 15, 1904, the *General Slocum*, a paddlewheel steamer eerily burned off Long Island Sound, N.Y. under very similar circumstances as the *Marine City*. There were approximately 1300 passengers and a crew of 35 aboard at the time. The death toll was 1,021, with most of the victims being women and children! During this tragedy, the fire hoses, pumps and life preservers were found to be defective and useless. The report from the investigating commission recommended that ships be built of metal, not of wood and that life preservers and fire hoses be made of materials that would not break down between inspections. Another recommendation was the use of frequent fire drills for the crew.[215] It is a sad fact that the very same reasons for the *Marine City* disaster were repeated so soon.

After the ruin of the *Marine City*, the steamer Pearl was placed on her route. [216]

[214] The Detroit Post and Tribune, Tuesday Morning, August 31, 1880
[215] Old News, David Vachon, February 2006, pages 8-10
[216] Alcona County Review, Friday, September 3, 1880

Inventory of Loss of a claimant in the Federal Court Records of a typical woman's suitcase on the *Marine City*

1.	One silk dolman[217]	25.00
2.	Cashmere winter shawl	17.00
3.	One lace shawl	20.00
4.	One lace parasol	25.00
5.	One velvet skirt	25.00
6.	Embroidered cashmere dress	25.00
7.	Bunting polonaise	10.00
8.	Linen lawn dress	7.00
9.	One dress bonnet	12.00
10.	One hat, ladies	5.00
11.	Dozen suit underclothing	20.00
12.	½ dozen embroidered gowns	18.00
13.	½ dozen embroidered skirts	15.00
14.	½ dozen lisle thread hose	5.00
15.	½ dozen boys hose	3.00
16.	4 pairs ladies boots and slippers	10.00
17.	1 gold chain	45.00
18.	1 silver watch	10.00
19.	1 duchess lace set and fischer	25.00
20.	1 silk umbrella	4.75
21.	1 hand embroidered satin hair piece	6.50
22.	3 pairs kid gloves	3.75
23.	2 pair mitts	2.00
24.	1 all wool walking suit	25.00
25.	4 sets ladies underwear	8.00
26.	1 blue satin dressing smock	10.00
27.	1 opera flannel dressing smock	5.00
28.	1 victoria lawn embroidered	5.00
29.	1 boys cashmere dressing gown	5.00
30.	2 boys percale night gowns	1.00

---

[217] A dolman is a hussar's jacket worn over the shoulders. See pictorial to the right.

ADDITIONAL REFERENCE SOURCES

- Michigan, Microsoft® Encarta ® Online Encyclopedia 2005, http://enarcarta.msn.com
- Alcona County Register of Deeds
- Alexander, Jeff. *The Muskegon.* Michigan State University Press, East Lansing, MI, 2006
- Archdiocese of Detroit
- Barry, James P., Wrecks and Rescues of the Great Lakes, A photographic history, , 1981, Howell-North books, Burbank, CA
- Brown, Hon Merrill, Harrisville, MI. Magistrate
- Burton Archives, Detroit MI
- Captain Pearson, Alcona Beach
- Chester Daily Times, Chester, PA, August 31, 1880
- City of Marine City Archives
- Detroit Free Press
- Detroit News
- Detroit Post
- Dickens, Charles, *American Notes for General Circulation*
- Donahue, James, "Terrifying Steamboat Tales"
- Dossin Museum, Detroit, MI

- Eicher, Al, "The Way It Was, Remembering the Doctors who Made House Calls, Lakeshore Guardian, www.Lakeshoreguardian.com
- Flock, Erica, Alcona County Review and reporter
- Gauthier, Doris, <u>Alcona – The Lake Pioneers</u>
- Geno, Robert, Rogers City, MI
- Great Lakes Maritime Institute
- Historical Collections of the Great Lakes, Bowling Green State University, Ohio
- History of the City of Harrisville Centennial Year
- <u>Images of America – The United States Life-Saving Service in Michigan</u>
- Inflation Calculator, www.westegg.com/inflation
- Journals, Life Saving Station, Sturgeon Point
- Judge J. Russell Hughes, Probate Judge of Alcona County
- July 1958 Telescope, GLMI Journal
- Library of Congress
- Library of Robert L. Bunting and the Robert Lowell Bunting Foundation
- Lloyds of London, London, England
- Manitowoc County, Wisconsin Genealogy: Ships and Shipwrecks of Manitowoc County, and biographies, <u>www.2manitowoc.com</u> and

http://lake3.lakefield.net/~mtwcgenw
eb/biosR.html

- Mansfield, J.B.History of the Great Lakes, Vol. 2
- Maritime History of the Great Lakes, www.hhpl.on.ca
- McGreevy, Robert, Harbor Beach, MI www.mcgreevy.com
- Michigan History, Lansing, MI
- Michigan History Magazine and overview for teachers, "Introducing Michigan's Past."
- Michigan Lighthouses, John Wagner
- Milwaukee Public Library
- National Archives, Chicago, IL
- National Archives, Washington
- Point Aux Barques Lighthouse Society
- Post and Tribune of Alcona, 1880
- Quinlan, Maria, Lumbering In Michigan, www.michigan.gov
- Raymond, Oliver, "Shingle Shavers and Berry Pickers", copyright 1976
- Sarnia Observer, September 17, 1830
- Sawyer, Don and Bennett, Gordon Alcona Historical Society, 2004 and 2005 Presidents
- Schelley, Marie. *Alcona, a Ghost Town.* Central Michigan University, 1967; Clarke Historical Library, Mount Pleasant, Michigan

- Scott, C.W. *Alcona County, Michigan, a Favored Land*, 1932, Clarke Historical Library, Mount Pleasant, Michigan
- St. Joseph Traveler-Herald, Sept. 4, 1880
- Sterling, Elrita, M. *First Fifty Years of Harrisville*. Central Michigan University, 1967; Clarke Historical Library, Mount Pleasant, Michigan
- Sturgeon Point Museum
- Swayze, David, www.boatnerd.com, Great Lakes Shipwreck file
- Swenson, Helen. *Sturgeon Point Coast Guard Station*. Central Michigan University, 1967; Clarke Historical Library, Mount Pleasant, Michigan.
- The Great Lakes Vessel Enrollment Online Database, www.ship-wreck.com
- The Helena Independent, September 1, 1880
- The Oshkosh Northwestern, August 31, 1880
- Toledo Blade Newspaper, Erica Blake reporter
- US Coast Guard, "A Legacy: The United States Life-Saving Service" Dr. Dennis L. Noble
- Ward Shipbuilders
  - Williamsport, PA Price-Three Centel, August 31, 1880
- Wisconsin Maritime Historical Society

- www.geocities.com/svandenbosch/qry namej.html
- www.henryfordhealth.org/12779.cfm
- www.linkstothepast.com
- www.newspaperarchive.com
- Zimmerman, Mabel Harrisville, MI

A Psalm of Life
By Henry Wadsworth Longfellow

Tell me not in mournful numbers,
Life is but an empty dream!
For the soul is dead that slumbers,
And things are not what they seem.

Life is real! Life is earnest!
And the grave is not its goal;
Dust thou are, to dust thou returnest,
Was not spoken of the soul.

Not enjoyment, and not sorrow,
Is our destined end or way:
But to act, that each tomorrow
Find us farther than today.

Art is long, and Time is fleeting,
And our hearts, though stout and brave,
Still, like muffled drums, are beating
Funeral marches to the grave.

In the world's broad field of battle,
In the bivouac of Life,
Be not like dumb, driven cattle!
Be a hero in the strife.

Trust no Future, howe'er pleasant!
Let the dead Past bury its dead!
Act, -act in the living Present!
Hearth within, and God o'erhead!

Lives of great men all remind us
We can make our lives sublime,
And, departing, leave behind us
Footprints on the sand of time;

Footprints, that perhaps another,
Sailing o'er life' solemn main,
A forlorn and shipwrecked brother,
Seeing, shall take heart again.

Let us then be up and doing,
With a heart for any fate;
Still achieving, still pursing,
Learn to labor and to wait.

"When the Moon on The Lake is Beaming."

THE UNDINE BOAT CLUB,

Respectfully announce that they have chartered Ward's new and splendid side-wheel steamer

MARINE CITY,

and will give a grand

Moon-Light Excursion,

(weather permitting)

Wednesday Evening, July 17th.

The services of the Union Silver Band have been engaged, and it is expected that many will avail themselves of this opportunity to "trip the light fantastic toe."

The boat will leave the dock at the foot of Jefferson street at 7½ o'clock, P. M.

Tickets, - - - $1.00

To be had of Members of the Club and on the boat.   july15td

Toledo Blade
July 15, 1867

Compliments of Toledo Blade, July 15th 1867

166

Retail orders may be made at your favorite bookstore, museum or by accessing www.amazon.com.

Wholesale orders for bookstores and museums: You may order this book direct from the publisher in quantities of ten or more by sending an e-mail to blackrivertradingcoltd@yahoo.com indicating inquiry is for a wholesale order.